THE SECRETS OF
D-DAY

LARRY COLLINS

Copyright ©2006 Larry Collins

All rights reserved. Written permission must be secured from the publisher
to use or reproduce any part of this book, except brief quotations in critical
reviews and articles.

ISBN: 1-59777-516-9

Library of Congress Cataloging-In-Publication Data Available

Book Design by: Sonia Fiore

Printed in the United States of America

Phoenix Books
9465 Wilshire Boulevard, Suite 315
Beverly Hills, CA 90212

10 9 8 7 6 5 4 3 2 1

TABLE OF CONTENTS

1. A Name for the Great Invasion 1

2. The Decision to Land is Made 7

3. Hitler Prepares for the Landing 17

4. "It Bloody Well Has to Work" 25

5. The Army of Ghosts 33

6. The Double Cross Committee 41

7. A Spaniard Code-named Garbo 49

8. De Gaulle Is Finally Let in on the Secret 59

9. Halcyon Plus Four 69

10. Rommel Heads Home 79

11. Verlaine's Sobbing Violins 89

12. A Flag for Sainte-Mère-Église 101

13. The Frenchmen of the SAS 111

14. The Miracle of D-Day—Surprise! 121

15. Omaha, Bloody Omaha 131

16. The Pointe du Hoc—Futile Heroism 143

17. D-Day—The Germans React 153

18. D-Day Night—All Still There To Play For 163

19. Liberation's Painful Price 173

20. Fortitude Plays its Cards 183

21. Hitler and the Germans Swallow Fortitude's Lie 195

1.

A Name for the Great Invasion

WHAT'S IN A NAME? In the years that have elapsed since the Normandy landings, the code word that covered the invasion—Overlord—has become engraved both on our hearts and in the pages of our history books. Where did it come from, this strange, nonsensical word? Why was it selected to cover the greatest western offensive of the Second World War? And who was responsible for choosing it?

How Overlord was picked as the invasion's code name is, indeed, one of the few amusing anecdotes in the serious, sometimes exalting, sometimes somber, often bloodstained history of that great operation. I thought I'd share the story of how it was chosen with you.

It goes back to early 1943 and the first headquarters established in London to begin drawing up a plan for the invasion. Its commander was an Englishman, General Sir Frederick Morgan. After several weeks of intense work, Morgan and his staff had finally completed their first, rough draft of a plan for breaking open the doors to the Continent. The time had come to submit it formally to Sir Winston Churchill, the British Prime Minister, and then to the Combined Chiefs of Staff.

Before doing that, however, Morgan had first to give it, in a sense, its formal baptism, to assign to the operation the code word which it would henceforth carry through the echelons of the Allied High Command and down through the pages of postwar history.

He called in one of his senior deputies, Major Roger Fleetwood Hesketh.

"I say, old boy," he said. "The time has come to give the great operation its code name. Do go around to ISSB and ask them what operational code words they have available for us to chose from."

ISSB—Inter Services Security Bureau—was the organization responsible for assigning and keeping track of all the code names for all of the Allies' secret operations anywhere in the world. It was a much more complex and important job than it might at first sound. Code names had to be carefully collated to avoid duplication. Those that might have been compromised had all been compiled so no similar sounding code names would be assigned to future operations. An effort was made to make sure code names that could be associated with each other—"knife" and "fork"—for example, weren't being used in the same geographical area.

Fleetwood Hesketh did as he was instructed. He went to the major commanding the ISSB in his secretariat at the War Office. "Look here," he said. "I've been ordered by General Morgan to bring back a code name for the great operation."

The officer dutifully measured the seriousness of Fleetwood Hesketh's request and went off to consult his books. He returned a few minutes later.

"I'm frightfully sorry," he told him, "but I'm afraid there's only one code word we have available at the moment."

"What's that?" Fleetwood Hesketh asked.

"MOTHBALL" the other officer replied.

Fleetwood Hesketh was aghast. "Are you absolutely certain?" he asked. "Operation Mothball seems rather a dreary code name for what is, after all, going to be our most important offensive in the West during this whole damn war."

"I'm frightfully sorry, old chap," the ISSB officer replied. "What with everything that's going on in the Pacific and the Mediterranean these days all the names we've selected and screened through our system have been spoken for. MOTHBALL's all I have left."

So, somewhat reluctantly, Fleetwood Hesketh took "Operation Mothball" back to General Morgan.

"Oh dear me," Morgan said when he heard it. "I don't fancy taking that into Winston. He's not going to like Operation Mothball one bit."

"Still, it does seem to be the only name the ISSB can come up with," Fleetwood Hesketh assured him.

General Morgan sighed. "Then I suppose I shall just have to take it up to him and see what he says," and he set off for the Prime Minister's office with his plan and his code word. He was back in half an hour.

"What happened?" Fleetwood Hesketh asked.

"Just what I knew was going to happen," Morgan told him. "Winston went right through the roof. 'Do you mean to tell me that those bloody fools want our grandchildren 50 years from now to be calling the operation that liberated Europe "Operation Mothball?"' he shouted. "'If they can't come up with a better code name for our landing than that, I'll damn well pick the code name myself.'

"Churchill," Morgan said, "glowered for a moment, pointed his cigar towards the ceiling, then reared back and barked: "'Overlord. We shall call it Overlord.'"

And that, indeed, is how the landings which liberated France and the rest of Occupied Europe came to be known before posterity as Operation Overlord and not, as a military bureaucrat suggested, as Operation Mothball.

The Allies knew those landings were a risk-filled enterprise; if they failed there was no way another assault on the Continent could be staged before the spring of 1945. That would have meant another year of occupation and privation for France and the rest of Hitler's conquests. Ten million, not six million Jews might have died in the gas chambers of the Holocaust had the invasion failed. The full weight of the Wehrmacht would have been turned on the Soviets once again. Could those brave people, bled white by three years of war, hold out? Or would they have had to sue for a separate peace? And, ultimately, one must ask—had the Normandy landings failed, would the atomic bombs that fell on Hiroshima and Nagasaki have fallen instead on Berlin and Munich?

So much was at stake in Normandy for the Allies that their Commander, General Dwight Eisenhower, vowed "We cannot afford to fail."

Yet, Hitler was determined they would.

For Hitler, defeating the landings and holding onto France was vital if he was going to have any hope of winning the war, or at least forcing it to a stalemate. His generals, he sneered, wanted to hold onto France so they could go on living in their requisitioned chateaux, drinking their fine wines, taking their mistresses to the nightclubs of Pigalle.

Hitler had to hold on to France to make war. What good were his V1 and V2 weapons, soon to come into full production, going to do him without their launching sites in the Pas-de-Calais? How would he range them on London and the rest of England without those bases? Without Brest and Saint Nazaire, how were his new silent submarines going to slink out into the Atlantic

Roosevelt and Churchill in 1943 on the portico of the Russian Embassy during the Tripartite Political Meeting of the Tehran Conference, November 28-December 1, 1943.

sea lanes? What good would his ME262 jet fighter be if he lost his advance warning radar stations in France? The coming invasion was an opportunity for the Fuhrer, not a threat—and an opportunity he was determined to seize.

2.

The Decision to Land is made

THE FINAL, IRREVOCABLE decision to invade the Continent of Europe was taken by the Allied High Command at the Hotel Chateau Frontenac in Quebec on August 15, 1943. The entire operation was assigned the codename Overlord. The landings were given the codename Neptune. May 1, 1944, was set as the target date for the landings. They would take place, the Allied Combined Chiefs of Staff decided, not in the Pas-de-Calais as the German High Command so confidently expected, but over the wide Norman beaches from which William the Conqueror had set out for England in 1066.

Why Normandy? Why didn't the Allies follow the dictates of conventional military wisdom and invade the Pas-de-Calais?

Part of the answer to that question lies in a basic and sometimes bitter difference in strategic thinking between the British and American general staffs. The

British strategic concept came down to one basic princi-
ple articulated again and again by Winston Churchill:
defeat the enemy by stealth, by weakening and harassing
his flanks, not by hitting him head-on where he was
strongest. Defeat him with guile, not by the reckless
squandering of men and machines. A legion of ghosts
dictated that British thinking, the ghosts of a generation
of Englishmen slaughtered in the bloody massacres of
the Somme.

No such ghosts troubled the sleep of America's
generals. The spirits which might have disturbed their
rest were a century old, the dead of the Civil War
Battlefields of Shiloh and Antietam. Strike head-on, the
Americans urged, hurl mass on mass in a frontal attack in
northwestern France, then smash on to the Ruhr Basin
and Germany's industrial heartland.

Any hope the American general staff had of
imposing that doctrine on their English allies had been
destroyed in one of the bloodiest defeats the Allies suffered in Western Europe, the ill-fated Anglo-Canadian
raid on Dieppe on August 15, 1942. Six thousand men
came ashore at dawn that day; by 0930 half of them were
casualties, the rest ordered to stage a humiliating with-
drawal. By five o'clock the shops along the city's waterfront were already re-opening for business.

That disaster would become a determining factor
in the Normandy landings. Victory at Dieppe convinced

the Germans of two things. First, it showed them that they could defeat an invasion at the water's edge, on the landing beaches. Second, it led them to conclude that the first objective of a future Allied landing would be the capture of a major seaport. Therefore, the key to defending *Festung Europa* was to build up impregnable beach defenses and to concentrate those defenses in the areas near the Channel ports: Boulogne, Dunkirk, Le Havre, Calais, Antwerp.

The Germans had gotten it completely wrong. For the Allies, the lessons of Dieppe were exactly the opposite of those the Germans had thought they would be. To the Allies, Dieppe was proof that no Allied landing was going to be able to capture a major seaport without appalling losses and giving the Germans all the time they needed to destroy the port's shipping facilities.

But if Dieppe had taught the Allies they couldn't hope to land the supplies to support their invasion through the docks of a captured port, how then were they going to get those supplies ashore? After all, the rules of warfare dictated that the success of a seaborne assault came down to one fundamental equation—would the attacker be able to reinforce his bridgehead by sea faster than the defender could bring up forces to assault it by land?

They would have to forget about a seaport, the Allies concluded, and find a way to supply their landing forces over the open invasion beaches. And not for just a few days. For weeks, certainly, perhaps for months. What the Allies would to have to do, said Admiral Lord Louis Mountbatten, the senior commander of the landings at Dieppe, is "find a way to bring a port along with us in our baggage."

Mountbatten found an answer to this problem as a consequence of the carnage of Dieppe. It was a massive artificial dock called the Mulberry. When Mountbatten first presented the idea to Churchill's planning staff, he was regarded as "having taken leave" of his senses. Yet those enormous concrete caissons would turn out to be the linchpins of the Allies invasion strategy.

Two were built, one for the American beaches, one for the British. Each contained two million tons of concrete and steel, required the labor of 10,000 men for eight months, cost almost $100 million, and could handle 12,000 tons of cargo a day, equal to the daily capacity of the Channel seaport of Dover. So enormous were those harbors that all the tugboats in England couldn't get them from Scotland, where they were built, to Normandy. Additional tugs had to be brought in from the Eastern Seaboard of the U.S. They would be towed to Arromanches after the beachhead had been established, then sunk off the shore where they were designed to rise and fall with the tides. To protect them from high seas, a ring of old merchant vessels would be scuttled in front of them as an artificial breakwater.

With the Mulberries, the Allied planners were freed from the imperative of landing near a major port. Now, they could avoid coming ashore in the places where the German defenses were strongest. A whole range of possible landing sites became available to them. There were, of course, still compelling reasons for landing in the Pas-de-Calais—the area's proximity to the Allies' strategic objective, the Ruhr, and the additional time fighter support could stay in the air over the beachhead.

However, an exhaustive study of the beaches along the Pas-de-Calais revealed that there were only four large enough to be assaulted by an infantry division. Furthermore, the area just inland from each of those beaches could be easily flooded and thus made impassible for Allied armour. Plus, they were exposed to the Channel's prevailing winds, getting the full brunt of its notoriously bad weather.

Those factors were what finally ruled out the Pas-de-Calais as a landing site. The Allied planners turned their attention to Normandy. German defenses were lighter there. The beaches running west from Caen were long, open swaths of land that could take the assault of several divisions. Indeed, they would offer the final plan almost 70 kilometers of open beaches, many of them sheltered from the Channel's prevailing winds. The terrain inland, hedgerow and *bocage* country, was made for the foot soldier, not the tank commander. That was going to slow down the build-up and breakout of the Allies armoured divisions. But that terrain would also hinder the Germans' efforts to hit the beachhead with a massive Panzer counter-attack.

Normandy, the final report that selected the invasion site noted, "suffers from the disadvantage that a considerable effort will be required to provide adequate air support for our assault and some time must elapse before the capture of a major port." But the other arguments were so overwhelming they left no choice: the Allies had to come ashore in Normandy.

The man who was to lead the whole gigantic enterprise, a 54-year-old former farm boy from Kansas named Dwight David Eisenhower, arrived in London to take up his command just after New Year's Day, 1944. He set up his personal headquarters at Hayes Lodge, a few minutes away from his headquarters in Grosvenor Square. Everything about Eisenhower—except for his infectious grin—was understated. Other Allied commanders might be given to wearing black berets or shiny helmets or carrying pearl-handled revolvers on their hip to set themselves apart from their fellow generals. Ike never wore anything but a simple uniform jacket with the four stars of his rank on his shoulders and a single row of ribbons. His calm, confident exterior concealed, however, a worried and driven man. He was smoking three packs of cigarettes a day.

His mission was defined in one. terse paragraph: "You will enter the Continent of Europe and, in conjunction with the other United Nations, undertake operations aimed at the heart of Germany and the destruction of her armed forces."

At about the same time Ike arrived, the man who would command his ground forces, Field Marshal Sir Bernard Montgomery, the victor of El Alamein, was setting up his headquarters at Saint Paul's School, in whose London lecture halls he had once conjugated Latin verbs and pondered the mysteries of the isosceles triangle. He proceeded, with Eisenhower's blessing, to rip apart the landing plan that had been prepared for them by General Sir Frederick Morgan. Monty said the Norman front on which Morgan planned to land was too narrow, the assault waves were lacking in firepower and depth. He said they must extend the beaches and add at least one more division to the landing force.

"That simply couldn't be done," Morgan's Anglo-American planners replied. The Allies didn't have the resources or the shipping to do what he wanted.

"Get them," Monty barked, "or get a new commander."

They did. The landing area was extended to go to the north to what became Utah beach; the first wave would now be composed of six, not four infantry divisions, with the addition of the veteran U.S. 4th and 1st Divisions. Basically, the invasion plan as it was finally worked out at Monty and Ike's headquarters called for four Allied Corps to filter into France through five beaches, Utah and Omaha for the Americans, Gold, Juno, and Sword for the British and the Canadians. The landings would be preceded on D-Day eve by a three-division airdrop: both the 82nd and 101st American landing on the Cotentin at Ste Mère-Église to secure the invasion's western flank along the Merderet River and the 6th British Airborne dropping astride the Orne River between Caen and the sea to secure the eastern flank.

D-Day had been set for May 5. Now, with the decision to strengthen the landing and lengthen the landing area, the date for D-Day had to be postponed for at least a month Picking a new date was for Eisenhower and his staff as challenging an operation as assembling a fine Swiss watch.

The first concern was for the airborne troops. They needed moonlight in the two hours after midnight if they were to locate the landmarks that would point them to their drop zones. For the assault troops, high tide would be the ideal time to land. They would have less ground to cover crossing the beach and therefore be less exposed to enemy gunfire in the opening phase of their assault. However, high tide was out as the water would cover the flowers in Rommel's Devil's Garden, the mines fixed to the tips of their wooden stalks. It would be impossible for the demolition engineers to find and disable them.

On the other hand, the troops couldn't land at low tide either, because at some beaches they would have to struggle through long tidal flats under murderous fire before reaching the sheltering bluffs behind the beach.

Finally, after wrestling with that problem for days, the planners decided H-hour would have to be set at precisely three hours before high tide. But should it be in daylight or in pre-dawn darkness?

"Daylight," argued the air and naval commanders. They needed at least an hour of daylight for their bombardment of the beaches if their bombing and naval gunfire was going to have the impact it was supposed to have. Balancing out all those factors left Eisenhower with just three days on which all the elements required for a landing would be in place, June 5, 6, or 7. He picked Monday June 5 as D-Day. H-hour was set for 0625 on Utah Beach, where the tide ran 30 minutes early, and 0645 on the other beaches.

The landing he would launch would be, without any question, the most complex, the most difficult, and the most dangerous military operation of the war in Europe. Almost 200,000 men would make the assault on D-Day. Over 5,000 ships, the largest armada ever to furrow the ocean's surface, would take them to Normandy and cover their assault with naval gunfire. Even Josef Stalin, who had so long despaired of ever seeing a second front in Western Europe, felt compelled to cable Eisenhower, "My colleagues and I cannot but admit that the history of warfare knows of no other similar undertaking from the point of view of its scale and its vast conception."

Vast and unprecedented it was. And yet, the success of that great armada might well be said to have depended not on gunfire and explosives, but on the guile of a little-known group of men and women laboring in an underground office in Winston Churchill's London headquarters.

Long lines of American soldiers moving inland on the French invasion coast in the D-Day assault; men and supplies come ashore following half-tracks and a beached 'duck' (amphibious truck). June 6, 1944.

3.

Hitler Prepares for the Landing

THE IMPRESSIVE PARADE, the 2.3 liter Mercedes Benz Cabriolet 230 of Field Marshal Erwin Rommel and the open Horch command car of Gerd von Rundstedt rolled past the towering fir trees, along the cliffs with their spectacular vistas of the valley below, up to the parking area at Wendeplatte 5610 feet into the Obersalzburg mountains. There, the marshals and generals started down the long tunnel carved into the mountain's granite to the high-speed elevator waiting to whisk them to Hitler's Eagle's Nest. At every 10 feet along their passage, a black-uniformed member of Hitler's personal bodyguard, the SS Liebstandarten, stood watch.

It was March 19, 1944. Hitler had summoned these men to the mountaintop hideaway, in which once he had schemed to conquer the civilized world, for a strategy conference that would decide how to preserve what remained to him of that world his armies had conquered, to plan how to reverse the fortunes of war, and save his

Reich for the thousand-year reign for which he had destined it.

There is no doubt that on that March morning, Hitler still believed all that was possible. Germany still had ten million men under arms mustered into over 3000 divisions. His factories were producing more arms than they'd turned out in 1940. They also were beginning to turn out his secret weapons—the V1 and V2 pilotless bombers and rockets that would soon begin to deliver their enormous high-explosive warheads on England's cities; the world's first jet fighter plane, the ME 262; and the Type 21 submarine, which would be able to stalk the Atlantic sea lanes undetected by Allied sonar.

The Führer's SS Aide-de-Camp Richard Schulze Kossens, one of the few who dwelt in his intimate inner circle, knew Hitler relished the prospect of the coming battle—that he was sincerely convinced he could win it—that he genuinely believed it would prove to be the turning point of the war.

The Field Marshals and generals he'd summoned to his Eagle's Nest held sway over ten million men, but at Hitler's headquarters they waited on the Fuhrer's pleasure. As each man arrived he was ushered into an ante-room where he could admire Hitler's collection of Nymphenburg and Frankenthal china. It was only when they had all assembled that Hitler's adjutant, General Rudolph Schmundt, ushered them all into the leader's presence.

Hitler was wearing a simple gray double-breasted tunic decorated with the Iron Cross Second Class he had won at Ypres, his subtle way of making clear to the beribboned gentlemen before him that while they might proudly clutch their silver Field Marshals' batons in their hands, they were still taking their orders from a former corporal.

The leader standing before those generals was both a physically and spiritually diminished man. He was suffering from severe cramps and gastric disorders and—although he did not know it—from advancing coronary sclerosis. His personal physician, Dr. Theo Morell, was prescribing him no less than 23 different medicines for those stomach troubles.

He greeted each officer individually, reserving a wide smile for those—Rommel was one—that he liked personally. Then he ushered them all into lunch in the Eagle's Nest sitting room.

Meals with Germany's Fuhrer were always a frugal and lugubrious affair. He, of course, was a vegetarian. The only thing he drank was a gaseous mineral water called Fachingen that was supposed to be good for his kidneys. His guests were fed very basic and uninspired German food—pork chops and red cabbage were a favorite of his kitchen. There was wine for those who wanted it. Dessert was fruit. His SS aide maintained Hitler always delighted watching a white-jacketed SS waiter place one shiny red apple before the Wehrmacht's great gourmet, Field Marshal von Rundstedt. Coffee, the Fuhrer's coffee, was the high point of the meal. It was Arabian coffee brought in once a year by submarine from Istanbul, at great risk, through the Straits of Gibraltar. The Fuhrer's guests may have been Field Marshals, but they still got only one cup of his coffee. No more.

When they'd all been served, Hitler began their strategy review. Almost immediately he brightened, some of his old vitality returned. He began by contemptuously dismissing the fighting abilities of the Anglo-American forces. He had little regard for the British soldier; none at all for the Americans. The Allies had won in the Mediterranean only because they had had the help of traitors, he declared. They would have no traitors helping them in the coming landings. They would find themselves up against battle-hardened German troops, behind near-impregnable fortifications. He welcomed the invasion, he declared. It was the great opportunity for which all Germany had been waiting. Then he turned to his Field Marshals for their assessment of the Allies' strategy in the coming clash.

For once, there was a rare unanimity among those men. The Allies would land in the Pas-de-Calais, across the Channel straits from Dover, along what had been the historic route from England to the Continent for centuries. Every bit of military logic and strategy dictated a landing there. There the Allies' landing craft would have only 20 miles of open water to cross. They could make five crossings from Dover to Calais for every trip they could make from southwestern England to Normandy or Brittany.

But above all, there were three compelling reasons why Eisenhower's planners had to choose the Channel Coast for their landing. Their first objective would have to be the seizure of a major seaport. Without a great port at their disposal, how could they hope to build up their beachhead with the troops, the vehicles, the massive tonnage in supplies and munitions they would need to sustain it? With the exception of Brest and Cherbourg, the great seaports were all concentrated along the Channel Coast.

For the Allies, the key to success would be their control of the air. That was the one area in which their dominance was overwhelming. In deciding where to land, they would inevitably choose the location in which they could maximize that critical advantage of theirs. There was no doubt where that was the Pas-de-Calais. The effective range of an RAF Spitfire was 150 miles. No sooner would one of those planes get over a Norman beachhead from a base in southeastern England than the pilot would have to turn around and head back to his base. In the Pas-de-Calais, he could prowl at his leisure seeking out German targets on the ground. The Americans' P51 had long-range fuel tanks that would allow them to be employed more effectively, covering a landing in

Normandy or Brittany. But over Calais they could roam the skies above the beachhead for hours.

Finally, all the marshals pointed out, if the Allies succeeded in breaking the Germans defensive lines in the Pas-de-Calais, they would have a wide, flat plain, ideal for tank warfare open before them, a plain that stretched like a dagger to the Ruhr and the heart of Germany's industrial machine. If the Allies were successful in landing in the Pas-de-Calais, von Rundstedt warned in the kind of prophecy only he would dare utter in Hitler's presence, then "the war would be over by Christmas."

Was there some wishful thinking in the predictions of the Field Marshals to go along with the wisdom of Clausewitz? Probably. The Atlantic Wall along the Channel Coast was, indeed, a formidable obstacle. It was there that those generals could feel most confident about defeating the invasion.

Hitler had long shared his generals' views. That was, after all, why he had begun building his Atlantic Wall in 1941. In November, 1943, he had predicted in his Directive No. 51 that the enemy "must and will attack" in the Pas-de-Calais to neutralize the launching pads of the V weapons with which he would soon be bombarding England. Now, suddenly, he was no longer so sure.

The German leader, his SS Aide-de-Camp said, liked to try to fit himself into the frame of mind of his adversary, to reason as his enemy would. Churchill and the English, he knew, liked to employ the indirect approach in their seaborne landings. Hadn't they used that approach in North Africa, in Sicily, Salerno, and at Anzio? Why would they change now for the most critical operation of the war?

His generals, he decreed, were wrong, prisoners of their overly rigid military logic. The Allies were not going to land on the Channel Coast. "The most threatened areas," Hitler announced in a stunningly accurate reading of the Allies' intentions, "are the two peninsulas, Brittany and the Cotentin." That is where the Allies would be tempted to land because they offered "the best possibilities" of establishing bridgeheads that could be expanded for their thrust across France.

And of the two peninsulas, the Cotentin was clearly the more attractive. It possessed the great port of Cherbourg. Its beaches and its landscape were more suitable than the harsher landscapes of Brittany. And once established there, the Allies would have a shorter distance to cross in their dash for the Ruhr.

First, he reiterated his order that all the great seaports on the French coast were to be considered fortress garrisons, to be defended to the last, then destroyed.

Wherever the Allies landed, he concluded "destroying the landing would be the sole decisive factor in the whole conduct of the war and hence the war's final result."

On their success or failure in defeating the landings, he declared, "depends the outcome of the war and the fate of the Reich."

Dwight Eisenhower giving orders to American paratroopers in England on June 6, 1944.

4.

"It Bloody Well Has to Work"

NOT QUITE 60 YEARS ago, at 1430 on Wednesday, May 10, 1944, a small group of Anglo-American officers gathered in Room 100A of the Combined Chiefs of Staff Building just off Grosvenor Square in London's Mayfair district. They were the members of the Combined Intelligence Committee and they were there that afternoon to hear General Eisenhower's latest estimate of how Hitler and the German General Staff would react to the forthcoming invasion.

Each of the men in the room had been cleared to read the Top Secret Ultra intercepts of the German's wireless communications. Nobody had to tell them, therefore, how much importance Hitler attached to defeating the invasion. The struggle for Normandy was, after all, going to be the decisive battle of the Second World War in the west. For the Wehrmacht, it would be the last chance to reverse the fortunes of war and save Hitler and his Third Reich from the disaster looming on the horizon.

To brief them that afternoon, Eisenhower had sent his intelligence officer, Major General J.F.M. Whiteley, an Englishman. In the years since the Normandy landings, the notion of the longest day, of the Germans throwing the Allied invaders back into the sea at the water's edge on D-Day itself, has taken hold of the popular imagination. That notion is strategic nonsense. The Allies were going to get ashore. The Allied High Command knew that. So, too, did the German High Command. The question was, could they cling to their Norman beaches once they were ashore if Hitler hurled the full weight of his Panzer divisions in France at their beachhead?

Those Allied officers had assembled to answer that question. Whiteley began by dividing the period immediately following the landings into four phases. The critical one for both Hitler and the Allies, Whiteley estimated, was going to begin on the evening of D-Day plus two, approximately 60 hours after the first assault waves had landed in Normandy. All the troops in the Allies' first wave would be ashore by then. They would be weakened by the losses they'd suffered in their landing and hemmed into a relatively small beachhead, some of it undoubtedly under German artillery fire. Their ships would be heading back across the open waters to load more men and material. It was at that moment when the Allies' beachhead would be at its most vulnerable.

That was also the moment, Whiteley told his audience, "when Hitler will have to take the decision to go whole hog and risk everything on throwing us out of Normandy." Before that moment, he couldn't feel certain that Normandy was the whole show, that a second landing might not still be coming in some other area. But at that point, Whiteley said, "it's got to be neck or nothing and he must be prepared to sell out all the no longer vital areas in the west."

He would have to give the order that night to strip his other areas of all their available reserves and start them for Normandy. If he did that, Whiteley told his audience, then some time around D plus four or five, those units would have arrived on the battlefield. They would have regrouped and be ready to launch a major counter-attack. They should include, Whiteley estimated, seven Panzer divisions, seven field divisions, including two paratroop divisions, and half a dozen independent tank battalions.

That would be the "critical point in the struggle." The Allied shipping would still be back in the United Kingdom, loading the men and machines of the second wave reinforcements while on the evening of D plus five, the Allied beachhead would be looking at "the horrifying prospect of a full blooded counter-attack" by those massed Panzer divisions.

Reading Whiteley's briefing notes, Field Marshal Sir Alan Brooke, the Chief of the Imperial General Staff, glumly remarked, "no landing, however cleverly conceived, however skillfully executed, can survive a massive counter-attack by the forces available to Hitler. He has the armour and the troops to throw us back into the sea, of that there is no doubt."

General Omar Bradley's intelligence officer, who heard Whiteley's briefing, put it even more succinctly to Bradley's Aide-de-Camp, Major Chet Hansen. "If Hitler's Panzers come over the hill between D plus three and D plus seven," he said, "our invasion doesn't stand a chance in hell of succeeding."

However, they never came.

That they did not was very largely the handiwork of a tiny band of men, most of them British, not one of whom fired so much as a single pistol shot during the entire battle for Normandy. Theirs was a company so secret barely 300 people even knew it existed in 1944. Privately, they were referred to as "Churchill's band of amateur Machiavellis." Officially, they belonged to something called "The London Controlling Section," one of those innocuous phrases chosen because it said exactly nothing. The section, the LCS, was the brainchild of the master conniver of them all, Winston Churchill. They reported directly to Churchill through his personal Chief of Staff, General Sir Hastings Lionel Ismay. Churchill had personally handpicked the Section's commander, Colonel John Henry Bevan. The only thing military about Bevan, it was said, was the high gloss on his shoes—the best shine, his admirers claimed, in the British Army. He wasn't even a career soldier; he was a London stockbroker of enormous wealth and impeccable breeding.

Bevan had gone to the right schools—Eton and Christ Church, Cambridge—won military honors in the trenches of the Somme knew, or even better, was related to all the right people. He was, as an associate remarked, "a very senior boy indeed."

What Bevan and his LCS controlled was something called Strategic Military Deception. Deceiving the enemy both tactically on the battlefield and strategically was very largely the art of the British during the Second World War. The Americans simply didn't believe in it and certainly not when it came to an operation as enormous as the Normandy landings.

The British, however, had so often been outgunned and outmanned by their German foes, that they had had little choice but to revert to it if they were going to win. They'd fooled Rommel at El Alamein by building miles of roads that went nowhere, railroad depots that would never see a train, pipelines that would never carry a drop of petroleum, filling the ether with fake radio messages, laying down fake tank treads. In 1943, they had deposited the body of the Man Who Never Was on the Spanish seacoast, an attaché case full of documents handcuffed to his wrist indicating that the Allies' first 1943 offensive would strike Sardinia and not Sicily.

Fundamentally, deception in warfare is the deliberate misrepresentation of reality in order to gain a strategic advantage over the enemy. Such strategic deceptions can fall into two categories. The first is labeled an ambiguous deception. The idea is to assault the enemy with a blizzard of misinformation, multiplying all the options he must consider before taking action. Its aim is to paralyze his ability to move decisively with that bewildering array of options.

The second is more subtle and much more difficult to execute. It involves reducing the ambiguity the enemy faces. Instead of swamping him with disinformation, he is subtly fed information which will nudge him along the road towards one precise, attractive option—instead of making him indecisive, help him to be very decisive—and very wrong.

That was the challenge before Colonel Bevan and his band of deceivers. The codename for their deception scheme was Fortitude. Work had begun on it at the same time work had begun on planning the invasion itself. But it was the decision to land in Normandy that finally breathed life and fire into Bevan's task. It was much easier to nudge an enemy towards a course of action to which he was already inclined than it was to lead him to change course and move in a direction in which he was not inclined to go. And Bevan, of course, knew from the Ultra intercepts that the German General Staff's thinking was concentrated on the Pas-de-Calais.

A good deception expert, Bevan liked to say, was like a playwright. He had to make up a story then get his audience to believe it through his actors, his scenery, his props, his sound and lighting effects. He had a good little story prepared for Hitler and his generals. Its aim was to infect their minds with its credibility, to lead them into making a mistake—not just any mistake, but the one precise mistake that would lead them to fall into the trap Bevan had set for them.

The story was this: Normandy was just the first of *two* landings. Its purpose was to get the Germans to strip their reserves out of the Pas-de-Calais and hurl them at the Normandy bridgehead. Once that was accomplished, then the real landing would fall on their weakened rear, on the Pas-de-Calais. Believe that lie, and the Germans would immobilize in the Pas-de-Calais the divisions which might otherwise defeat the Allies in Normandy.

Indeed, Bevan's scheme would have made sound strategic sense for the Allies were it not for one vital fact—they barely had enough troops in the British Isles to stage one landing, to say nothing of two.

Nonetheless, he would have to slip that lie to his German foes, bit by bit, piece by tainted piece, through every means and channel he could find, until in a burst of inspiration, the Germans would assemble the jigsaw puzzle he'd set before them, convinced as they did that they were putting it together solely through a stroke of their own genius.

It was a staggeringly difficult task, so difficult that Field Marshal Sir Alan Francis Brooke told Bevan when they first discussed the idea, "It will never work—but it bloody well has to."

Allied landing on Omaha Beach, D-Day, June 6, 1944.

5.

The Army
of Ghosts

SIXTY YEARS AGO, all of southwestern England was an armed camp. From Land's End, through Cornwall, behind Portsmouth and Southampton, in the green valleys of Wales, the men and machinery of the invasion were assembled and waiting. Piles of ammunition crates were stacked 10 feet high under the leafy branches of oak and chestnut trees. Half-tracks, armoured cars, two-and–a-half ton Dodge trucks, Sherman tanks lined up bumper to bumper as far as the eye could see, ready to embark for the Norman shore. So many new airfields—163—had been built for the coming invasion that the pilots joked you could taxi your aircraft from one end of England to the other without ever scraping a wingtip.

On the other side of the Thames, in Kent, Sussex and East Anglia, in the rich and fertile farmlands behind the White Cliffs of Dover, the scene was everywhere repeated. Olive drab army tents, their flaps billowing in the spring breeze, their cook-stoves pumping smoke into the May skies, stretched along the hills and into the hidden valleys. Here, too, were thousands of neatly stacked wooden ammunition crates, mountains of jerry cans, row on row of Sherman tanks concealed beneath the protective awning of their camouflage netting.

Only one thing set those encampments speckling the countryside of southeastern England apart from their sister encampments on the other side of the Thames.

There were no troops inside those tents.

There was not a single round of ammunition in those wooden crates.

There was not a drop of gasoline in those jerry cans.

Those Sherman tanks were made not of steel but of rubber. They were as harmless as the balloons at a child's birthday party.

They all belonged to an army of ghosts. That phantom army was the proudest creation of Colonel John Bevan, the British officer who was responsible for Fortitude, the plan designed to deceive the German High Command about the Allies' real intentions on D-Day.

But there was a problem with that plan—troops. There were barely enough men and machines in England to stage one invasion, to say nothing of two. How were the Germans ever going to swallow Fortitude's lie if they weren't first convinced the Allies had enough forces in England to stage two full invasions?

Those deserted tent cities were Colonel Bevan's answer.

He didn't have the troops. He'd make them up. He would create an army of ghosts and populate the fields of southeastern England with his phantoms. He gave his imaginary army an imposing name—The First United States Army Group, FUSAG. He assigned it a commander, General George S. Patton, the aggressive tank commander the Germans believed would lead the invasion. The army had its headquarters at Wentworth, near Ascot. It was composed of two real armies, the 1st Canadian Army and the 3rd U.S. Army, and real infantry and armoured divisions. The only thing was, those divisions weren't in England—they were all still in training back in the United States and Canada.

"The whole idea's a pile of rubbish!" exclaimed Major Ralph Ingersoll when he was assigned to help Bevan implement the Fortitude plan. "It's crazy, crazy, crazy. The Germans will never believe it."

Yet if they did, it was going to be in large part thanks to a flash of genius Ingersoll had on one of his first assignments for Colonel Bevan. He was detailed to inspect the factory where skilled British carpenters, working meticulously to scale, were making wooden models of Sherman tanks to serve as decoys for German reconnaissance flights. Trouble was, Ingersoll noted, it took almost as much time to build a fake tank as it did to build a real one.

Then, suddenly, he remembered the Macy's Thanksgiving Day Parade in New York and its huge rubber floats of Mickey Mouse and Donald Duck. Why not make their tanks of rubber? Forty-eight hours later Ingersoll was at the Pentagon in Washington presenting his idea to the representatives of the five leading tire manufacturers in the United States. In a month-and-a-half, his Sherman tanks, along with Dodge trucks and light and heavy pieces of field artillery began to pour into England. They came in packages no bigger than a suitcase.

"Imagine," Ingersoll chortled, "a Sherman tank in a suitcase!"

Hook them up to an air compressor, however, and they ballooned out into imitations so complete there were even rivets on their turrets. A hundred tanks could be set out in the fields of southeastern England in a night, while one real tank tore apart some poor farmer's fields to leave behind the treads the rubber tanks should have made. The scene was carefully covered by a camouflage net—but not so carefully that an adventuresome Luftwaffe reconnaissance pilot couldn't get an indication of what the netting concealed.

To breathe life into those phantom units, a special detachment of U.S. Army Signal Corps troops was sent to England. Their mission: imitate in exact detail all of the wireless messages Fortitude's army of ghosts would be sending out if they really were moving into position in southeastern England. Some were in code. Some were in the clear. Some were by Morse, some were by voice transmission. Former Broadway and Hollywood actors that could imitate every American accent from a Maine twang to a Brooklyn snarl did the voice transmissions. Seventeen teams of 10 men each put out the radio messages. Some moved around southeastern England in mobile vans. Others were permanently stationed in those villages where the Germans were supposed to believe the major commands of Fortitude's army of ghosts were located.

It was all a charade, of course, but it was a deadly serious charade. And, if it was going to work, Fortitude's army of ghosts would have to take on flesh and blood where it mattered most, not in that tranquil English countryside, but in the minds of the German General Staff and ultimately, in the mind of Adolf Hitler himself. The first stop on the journey to Hitler's mind was a building called Maybach I, in the city of Zossen, 20 miles from Berlin. Zossen was the wartime headquarters of the German Army's High Command. There with their privileged rations, their Viennese Haut Ecole horses, Hitler's senior officers lived out the rituals of their Junker caste disdainfully immune to the sufferings of the world their armies had devastated.

Maybach I was the office of *Fremde Heere West*— Foreign Armies West—the branch of the Wehrmacht responsible for assessing the Allies' strength in the west and estimating for Hitler how the Allies would employ that strength in the coming struggle. Its commanding officer was Colonel Alexis Freiherr Baron von Roenne. Von Roenne was as much a Teutonic aristocrat as his enemy, Fortitude's commander Colonel Bevan, was an Anglo-Saxon one. His Prussian forbears had received their baronetcy at the hands of Frederick the Great himself.

But most important, Hitler believed in von Roenne and his work. He had had his eyes on the austere Prussian since August 1939 when von Roenne had gone against the wisdom of his seniors and assured the Fuhrer that the French and the English armies would not budge beyond the Maginot Line while his legions swept through Poland. Hitler himself had hand-picked von Roenne for his critical assignment in late 1943.

Von Roenne's task had never been an easy one, but as the invasion season drew closer, it became much more difficult. The problem was Hermann Goering and his Luftwaffe. Goering was no longer willing to risk his dwindling supply of aircraft on reconnaissance missions. That gap left von Roenne with two primary sources of information, wireless intercepts and the reports of the Abwehr's agents in England. The meticulous von Roenne's experience had led him to be wary of the reports of German agents behind the Allied lines or in contact with Allied diplomats in neutral capitals.

If he was going to have to depend on them, then von Roenne decided he would have to ask Admiral

Wilhelm Franz Canaris, the head of the German intelligence service, for his personal evaluation of those agents.

There were two, Canaris told him, in whom he could have complete confidence. Both were operating from England. One was a Pole. His codename was Vertrauensmann—V-Mann, or secret agent—Armand. The other was a Spaniard. His codename was V-Mann Arabal.

Roenne had every reason to be grateful to those two men. As the invasion drew closer and the Luftwaffe's aerial reconnaissance dwindled to virtually nothing, he had had to attach ever growing importance to the information they furnished him.

Fortunately, von Roenne's files survived the war. The key one, NR2796/44, the Weekly Estimate of Allied Intentions and Strength, was prepared for Hitler's headquarters on May 15, 1944. It relied heavily on the reports Armand and Arabal had sent their Abwehr controllers in the first two weeks of May. There were, von Roenne estimated, a total of 78 Allied divisions in England that day. The focal point of the Allies' troop concentration in southeastern England, he continued, "becomes more and more marked." As far as the Allies' invasion strategy was concerned, "the main attack," he predicted, "must be expected on either side of the Pas-de-Calais."

There were, in fact, 37 Allied divisions in England that day. All but three of them were in southwestern England, opposite the Normandy and Brittany coasts. The architects of the Fortitude deception scheme could not have written a better report for Hitler and his generals themselves.

Coast Guard manned JSS LST-21 unloads British Army tanks and trucks onto a Rhino barge during the early hours of the invasion, June 6, 1944. Note the nickname "Virgin" on the Sherman tank at left.

6.

The Double Cross Committee

IT WAS TYPICAL of those resolutely dreadful Victorian buildings that once dominated central London—its red brickwork faded to the color of dead autumn leaves, the paint on its trim at least two decades old. The address, however—58 Saint James Street—was as fashionable as the building was dreary. Three letters written on the arch over the building's main entrance—MGM—identified the buildings' owners, Metro Goldwyn Mayer. In the years before the war, the Hollywood filmmakers had used the building as the European headquarters from which they distributed their celluloid fantasies throughout Europe.

Every Wednesday afternoon during the spring of 1944, a handful of Englishmen, some in uniform, some in civilian clothes, strolled discreetly into that building. Fantasies of a rather different sort than those produced by MGM were their concern. Their destination was the third-floor conference room of the building's primary wartime occupants, MI5, British Counter Intelligence. They belonged to what was known as the Twenty Committee for the double X Roman numerals by which the Committee was designated.

They were also referred to as the Double Cross Committee because the main concern of those men at their weekly meetings was double-crossing their German foes. All the Allies' secret organizations were represented on the Committee: MI6, the Secret Intelligence Service, the London Controlling Service, the American OSS (Office of Strategic Services, the wartime precursor of the CIA), the intelligence services of the army, the Royal Navy, and the RAF. Their chairman was an Oxford don John Cecil "J.C." Masterman, a gentleman of such portentous demeanor his colleagues joked his initials should really stand for Jesus Christ.

In that springtime of 1944, those men presided over the consequences of one of the most remarkable successes in the history of counter-espionage. There was that springtime not a single German agent operating from British soil—not one. The fact that there were none was due to the work of a wiry Scot, Colonel Thomas A. "Tar" Robertson. Since 1939, Robertson had been systematically rounding up German agents and playing them back against their Abwehr controllers either by their radios or by their written communications. Thanks to his penetration of the German networks, every time a new German agent attempted to slip into England from a submarine or was dropped by a Luftwaffe bomber, he was welcomed with open arms by Robertson's men.

By early 1942, it had become evident to Robertson that every agent the Germans had infiltrated into England was either dead, in jail, or working for him. The Double Cross Committee was formed to deal with the consequences of Robertson's stunning achievement.

Its task was to systematically play those agents back against their German controllers, to build up the Germans' confidence and trust in their work. That meant, of course, that most of the information the controlled agents were sending to the Germans—roughly 80 percent of it—had to be accurate. When the Germans asked specific questions, they had to be given answers, and in most cases the right answers.

Many an innocent English man or woman paid with their lives for that operation when the Luftwaffe bombed targets the Double Cross Agents had identified for them. It was, alas, a part of the dreadful price of giving those agents the credibility they needed if they were going to be able to pass on to their German controllers the lies that could change the course of the war.

And, indeed, by the eve of the Normandy Invasion, those innocent victims had been avenged. The operation was ready to pay the Allies enormous dividends. First, there were no German agents in England who could get into the fields of Kent or Sussex to discover the hoax the British were preparing with their imaginary First U.S. Army Group.

But much more important, it meant the agents whose stature had been so carefully nurtured with their Abwehr controllers could now be used to slip into the Germans' eager hands bits and pieces of the jigsaw puzzle that would point the thinking of Hitler and his generals in just the direction the Allies wanted it to go in the hours after the Normandy landings.

Two of those agents would be critical in doing that job—a Pole and a Spaniard. They were the two agents whose work and whose reports, Admiral Wilhelm Canaris had informed the head of the German Army's Intelligence branch, could be regarded as completely reliable.

The Pole was a Polish Air Force officer, a crack pilot and a pre-war Olympic skier named Roman Czerniawski. His adventure had begun, curiously enough, in a cell in Fresnes Prison.

Czerniawski had fled to France after the Germans had ravaged his native Poland in September 1939. There, he fought the Germans yet again as a volunteer with the French Army during the debacle in 1940. He managed to avoid capture and get back to Paris and immediately took up the anti-Nazi fight again, this time by organizing one of the first clandestine intelligence networks for the

British Secret Intelligence Service. It was called *Interallié* and it soon became a highly effective operation.

Czerniawski, alas, was much given to amatory adventuring. He soon developed a romantic liaison with his code clerk, a stunningly seductive lady named Mathilde "La Chatte"—the Kitten—Carre. She in turn was caught in a trap set by an agent of the Abwehr, Hugo Ernst Bleicher. Once caught, La Chatte focused her very substantial charms on Bleicher, became his mistress and betrayed her colleagues in the Resistance.

When Bleicher's boss, Colonel Oskar Reille, the head of the Abwehr in France, studied the operations of Czerniawski's *Interallié* network, he was shocked by how successful the group had been. The Abwehr, he knew, had nothing remotely like *Interallié* functioning in England. Hence his visit to Czerniawski in his Fresnes Prison cell.

Reille offered the Pole a classic *Godfather* offer. Go to England and spy for Germany, he told the Pole. If he agreed, Reille would see that the lives of the 63 Frenchmen and women who had been arrested along with Czerniawski were spared. They would become, in a sense, hostages to his loyally serving the Reich in England.

And if the Pole didn't accept Reille's offer?

Then he could go off to the gallows right along with his fellow Resistants.

Czerniawski chose England. The Abwehr arranged for an "escape" for him on Bastille Day, 1942.

By September equipped with instructions on how to make a shortwave radio set and a lengthy questionnaire to which Reille wanted answers, Czerniawski was in England. He immediately contacted MI5, told them what he'd done and pleaded for help in saving the lives of the members of his network.

The English were less than convinced—hence his English code name "Brutus." Still, out of concern for the 63 members of his intelligence network, they set him up in a house in Richmond Hill with a transmitter and a sergeant in the Royal Signal Corps as his radio operator, and then let him send a flow of third-rate intelligence information to Reille at the Hotel Lutetia in Paris. To their amazement, Ultra intercepts of Reille's radio messages to Berlin revealed the Germans were coming to regard Brutus as a first-class agent.

Why disappoint them, reasoned the English.

They gave Czerniawski a promotion. Since he was a Polish Air Force Officer, they made him the Free Polish Air Force Liaison officer to the RAF. And, once again, he shot up in the esteem of his Abwehr controllers.

With the spring of 1944 and the need to bring Fortitude into play, Brutus/Czerniawski suddenly became a godsend, a blessing from heaven to the men of the Double Cross Committee. They promoted him to Polish Liaison officer to their imaginary First Army Group. Because he was a serving officer, he could be logically expected to meet people, go to places, attend briefings, see and understand things which would be inaccessible to a civilian agent. As March, April and May 1944 unfolded, the Pole became for the Germans a priceless source of information—all of it false and all of it vital to the success of the coming invasion.

And the other Allied double agent? The Spaniard? His code name was Garbo—after the beautiful Swedish actress. And he was without a doubt the most important double agent of the war—more important than Stalin's Richard Sorge in Tokyo, or even Cicero, the German spy who posed as the butler of the British Ambassador in Turkey.

Wounded men of the 3rd Battalion, 16th Infantry Regiment, 1st Infantry Division, receive cigarettes and food after they had stormed Omaha Beach on D-Day, June 6, 1944.

7.

A Spaniard
Code-named Garbo

GARBO. WHAT IMAGE does that name evoke in our minds? Surely, the face of that beautiful and enigmatic Swedish film star who wanted to be left alone, Greta Garbo. Yet there is another image it might more appropriately evoke in the days leading up to the anniversary of the Normandy Landings. Unfortunately, it is an image without a face, that of the man who was without any doubt the most important double agent of the Second World War, a man whose work played a pivotal role in the success of the Allied landings.

His name was Juan Pujol Garcia—"Garbo" for the Allies he served so well—"Arabal" for the Nazis he betrayed with such devastating effectiveness. You will find no photographs of Garbo in the archives of the landing. For decades he lived under an assumed identity in a South American nation, ever fearful of the vengeance of those he once befriended and betrayed.

Garbo/Garcia's story is a fascinating one. He was a Spaniard, a Catalan from Barcelona and a fervent anti-communist who fought in Franco's Fascist Legions during the Spanish Civil War. That service left him with disgust for Franco's German and Italian allies. The only hope for Europe, he became convinced, lay in the liberal democracies of France and England. When France fell in 1940, he decided the time had come to take up a personal engagement in the conflict enveloping the West.

He went to the officer representing MI6 in Madrid and offered his services. Let him go to the local offices of the Abwehr, German Military Intelligence, he told the British. He would tell the Germans he was about to leave for England to work for a Spanish pharmaceutical firm and offer them his services as a spy. Because of his years in Franco's legions they would have no reason to doubt his attachment to the Fascist cause and sign him on. In reality, of course, he would be working for the Allies.

The MI6 officer who interviewed him saw "Abwehr entrapment" written across poor Garcia's forehead. He showed him the door with barely a minimum of courtesy.

That did not discourage Garbo. He went to see the Abwehr anyway. He was off to London, he told the man who interviewed him, and was prepared to become an agent for the great Nazi cause. The Germans proved a good deal more responsive than the English had been.

Garbo was introduced to the head of the Abwehr station, Erich Kuhlenthal, assigned a code name "Arabal," given training in the use of secret inks, funds, and a list of questions the Germans wanted answered. Then he was off for London.

Except there was a problem. Garbo had about as much chance of getting to England as he did of going to the moon. He went to Lisbon instead and set up shop there. As the basis for his reports to Kuhlenthal, he would employ the British press available in the Portuguese capital. But how was he going to explain to his Abwehr controller how his reports were getting from London to Madrid?

Garbo used his imagination. He made up a courier who could get those reports to Lisbon for him, an English friend, a steward who, he informed Madrid, worked on a ship sailing between Liverpool and the Portuguese capital. Each time the ship on which his imaginary steward was supposed to be working tied up in Lisbon, Garbo would drop into the mail a report to Kuhlenthal in the secret ink and the code he'd been assigned.

Those reports were nothing more than a fistful of smoke based on Garbo's reading of his English papers. But he was a perceptive man. He knew how to read between the lines and on occasion the information he furnished Kuhlenthal was embarrassingly close to the truth. Indeed, he became so good that British counter intelligence began to pick up traces of him reading their Ultra intercepts of the traffic between Kuhlenthal's Madrid base and the Abwehr's headquarters in Berlin. Who, they wondered, was this V-Mann Arabal operating with such apparent impunity on British soil?

After almost a year of freelance spying, Garbo/Garcia went back to MI6 in Madrid and identified himself as V-Mann Arabal. This time, the British were ready to give him a decoration. He was whipped back to England on the first available transport and assigned to MI5's controlled agent program.

As his control officer, he was assigned a diabolically clever Anglo-Spaniard named Tomás "Tommy" Harris. Harris, a world renowned expert on Goya and Greco, had acquired a fortune in the three years before the war selling Spanish art from the gallery on the ground floor of his sumptuous Mayfair town house. A few malicious tongues suggested that he was, in fact, providing an outlet for works stolen by his Loyalist friends from the Catholic churches in Republican Spain.

Harris was fascinated with Garbo's tactic of making up sub-agents to help him in his work—and that despite the fact one of Garbo's creations—a retired IRA gunman living outside Liverpool—was a bit of an embarrassment. The man was supposed to be living in an area where he could be expected by Madrid to record the arrival of incoming Allied transports. Garbo, Harris decreed, had imagined the man into existence; he could equally well imagine him into the grave. The poor chap contracted cancer of the pancreas, a rapidly fatal form of the disease and was dead before the first American troopship docked in Liverpool.

Harris and Garbo then set out over the next months to build themselves a first-class network of imaginary agents. For their recruits, they turned first to the army of Imperial malcontents sprinkled throughout England: Welshman, Sikhs, Greek Cypriots, Gibraltarians of Spanish descent, Egyptians. To them was added the inevitable Spanish communist who thought he was funneling information to the party in Madrid; the American sergeant who drank too much at Garbo's parties and unbuttoned his lips; the dowdy secretary in the Ministry of Information who was awed by Garbo's prowess as a Latin lover.

The whole thing had an Alice in Wonderland air to it. As each potential agent was spotted, Garbo would discuss his or her merits and drawbacks with Kuhlenthal. The German would suggest trial tasks to determine the potential recruits abilities. Some succeeded. Many did not and on Kuhlenthal's good counsel were dropped.

By February 1944, the Garbo network was composed of 24 of those wholly imaginary agents. Geographically, they had been given a slight but not suspicious tilt towards southeastern England where they could be employed to further the Fortitude plan. As

FUSAG's army of ghosts began to assemble, Garbo's agents started up a steady flow of information to Madrid. It was not information of the high military quality Brutus was providing his controller, but precise bits and pieces of information—the marking on an American halftrack seen in Kent; the design of a Canadian soldier's shoulder patch in East Anglia; the boast of a drunken GI in a Dover pub—all were designed to dovetail with Brutus's more technical information flow.

Then, in late April, 1944, Harris had a flash of genius. On the morning of D-Day, at roughly 0300, let his man Garbo inform Kuhlenthal in Madrid that the invasion was about to take place, he urged his superiors. Let Garbo radio the Germans that the invasion fleet had already sailed and that assault was imminent—and *let him do it before the first Allied soldier had stepped ashore in Normandy.*

Harris had worked out very carefully the time it would take for Garbo's message to be radioed to Madrid; the time Madrid would need to decode it, then re-code it and radio it to Berlin. Finally, he had factored in the time it would take Berlin to decode it again.

On the basis of those calculations, he knew that by the time Berlin had received Garbo's report, it would be too late to warn Germany's troops in Normandy. But how Garbo's reputation would soar in the eyes of his German controllers! After all, they would know that their man Garbo had gotten his message out of London *before* the troops had landed. Suddenly, he would have become the finest agent the Reich possessed anywhere in the world.

On the strength of that first, stunning success, Garbo would send off a second message 48 hours after the landing, at that critical point when Hitler would have to be making up his mind as to whether or not Normandy was the real invasion. Watch out, it would warn, a second attack is about to strike the Pas-de-Calais. Because Garbo had been so right with his first message, the Germans, Harris reasoned, would be more than well-disposed to believe his second one.

Everyone on the Double Cross Committee, which controlled the double agents, agreed it was a great idea. They also agreed Eisenhower would never accept it. To their surprise, however, he did.

Harris and Garbo had now to come up with a convincing explanation of just how Garbo was going to discover the secret of the invasion.

One of those imaginary agents of his, agent Number Four, a Spaniard previously living on Gibraltar and enjoying, as a consequence, a healthy dislike for his English neighbors, was working in the NAAFI cafeteria, the British Army's soldiers' canteen, in the Chislehurst caves. On April 27 he informed Garbo that he had been re-assigned to a new location and been made to sign the security certificate which all NAAFI employees assigned to the invasion assembly areas had to sign. Garbo immediately radioed this news to Kuhlenthal at Abwehr headquarters in Madrid.

Three days later, Four arranged to meet Garbo at the Winchester railroad station. He'd been assigned to Hiltingbury Camp where the 3rd Canadian Infantry Division was quartered. The camp existed; so, too, did the division. Indeed, it would lead the first wave ashore on Juno Beach on D-Day.

That night, Garbo informed Madrid of Four's new assignment.

Then, on May 5, Four got a sensational message out to Garbo: his Canadians had been given two days of cold rations, lifebelts, vomit bags for seasickness, and then had left camp. He'd been ordered to clean the camp, presumably for its next occupants. That could only mean one thing—the invasion was on!

Garbo immediately got the news off to Madrid in a triumphant message.

What had in fact happened is that the Canadians had, indeed, been issued all the equipment Four had detailed and embarked—to participate in a massive landing exercise, the last rehearsal before the invasion itself. It was an exercise so important the Germans were bound to see it—as indeed they did.

When the Canadians returned to camp after the exercise and a shamefaced Four communicated this bad news to Garbo, the Spaniard exploded in fury. They should sack the imbecile immediately, he radioed Madrid.

Kuhlenthal, undoubtedly aware that the landing exercise had taken place, counseled patience instead. Four's information had been exact. The error had been in the interpretation they had put on it. Praise poor Four rather than condemn him, Kuhlenthal urged, because the next time he spotted those vomit bags being passed out, it might mean the invasion really was coming.

The Abwehr general had reacted exactly as the English had hoped he would. He would be hearing about those vomit bags once again all right—on the morning of June 6 in a message that was going to have a substantial impact on the course of the war.

Troops in an LCVP landing craft approaching Omaha Beach on D-Day, June 6, 1944.

8.

De Gaulle Is Finally
Let in on the Secret

FOR CHARLES DE Gaulle, the climatic events of the Normandy landings and their promise of France's liberation should have been one of the most exalting moments of his life. They would represent the culmination of the long, hard crusade for his country's freedom on which he had embarked, almost alone, four years earlier.

They were not.

They brought him, in fact, some of the most painful and bitter moments of his life.

Less than 36 hours before the first Allied paratroops would drop onto the soil of France, the leader of the Free French hadn't even been informed that the invasion was about to take place, nor where it was going strike when it came.

There had even been some question as to whether or not de Gaulle himself should be brought to London from his headquarters in Algiers to be present in the British capital when the landings took place. Churchill insisted to a hesitant Roosevelt that he had to come and be made aware of the invasion before it actually took place. Anything else would be an unbearable insult to both de Gaulle and the French as a whole.

As a gesture of goodwill, once Roosevelt had agreed, Churchill sent his personal York airplane to Algiers to fly de Gaulle to England. The goodwill engendered by his action barely lasted the time of an aperitif. As soon as de Gaulle had showered and shaved at the Hotel Connaught, he was escorted to lunch with Churchill before joining him on his private train for the trip to Eisenhower's forward invasion headquarters at Southwick House, outside Portsmouth.

It was a very high-level lunch. De Gaulle's party included General Marie-Pierre Koenig, commander of all the Free French forces. With Churchill was South Africa's Field Marshal Jan Christian Smuts, Anthony Eden and his Labor Party ally, Ernest Bevin.

The English Prime Minister was in a foul temper. The weather was threatening the whole invasion scheme and he was in no mood to countenance de Gaulle's complaints and demands.

De Gaulle was in an equally vile frame of mind. Some weeks earlier the English had forbidden the French in London to communicate with Algiers in anything but an open cipher. They were afraid that someone might slip word of the invasion plans to Algiers. It was, as it turned out, a perfectly justified concern. Postwar examination of the Abwehr records would show that de Gaulle's Algerian headquarters had indeed been penetrated by the Germans.

De Gaulle, however, had read the gesture as a personal insult and yet another manifestation of the Anglo-Saxon's deep mistrust of the Free French. He had given General Koenig the order to withdraw all the French officers assigned as liaison personnel to the Allies' invading troops.

It was an appalling action, one even de Gaulle's close advisors felt was uncalled for. The Labor Leader Ernest Bevin exploded. Such a gesture would be an overtly hostile act towards the Allies.

De Gaulle dismissed him with haughty glance, reiterating his demand that he be allowed to communicate with Algiers in his personal cipher.

Churchill then struck right at the heart of the matter. Roosevelt was urging de Gaulle to go Washington and consult with him on the formation of a postwar government for France.

De Gaulle would as soon have gone to dinner with the devil. On the eve of his departure from Algiers, he had beaten the Americans to the punch. His Consultative Assembly had voted to change the name of his movement from the French National Committee of Liberation to the Provisional Government of the French Republic.

France already had a government, he told Churchill—*his* government. What was there to discuss in Washington? Besides, to him as a Frenchman it was totally unacceptable to discuss the internal political affairs of his nation with a foreign head of state, however friendly to France he might be.

The Allies, he pointed out, had recognized the Greek, Polish, and Yugoslavian governments in exile. Now they could recognize his government.

In reality, of course, de Gaulle was convinced Roosevelt was conspiring against him, trying to find a way to install someone else at the head of a postwar government in France.

His suspicions were entirely justified. Roosevelt had already given instructions to Allen Welsh Dulles, head of the Office of Strategic Services in Bern, Switzerland, to open contacts with Édouard Herriot as soon as possible. He was to persuade the pre-war Radical Party leader to become the American stalking-horse in an effort to depose de Gaulle as France's postwar Chief Of State.

Churchill's antipathy to de Gaulle was personal. The French leader's constant demands and complaints, along with his haughty demeanor, exasperated the Englishman. But politically, the two were close. Both foresaw the challenge communism was going to lay down to the postwar democracies in liberated Europe and wanted to prepare to meet it.

Roosevelt did not. Surrounded by friends and advisors of liberal perception, he tended to minimize the communist threat. He was inclined to see de Gaulle as the French leader's opponents on the left saw him, as a military autocrat lacking proper democratic—or, as the French would say, Republican—credentials.

For de Gaulle, what was at stake in these discussions was enormous. At issue, after all, was nothing less than the sovereignty and full independence of postwar France—to say nothing of his own destiny. For nothing in the world was he going to allow the Allies to install their hated AMGOT—Allied Military Government of Occupied Territories—on France as their armies advanced. Reduce France, the ally of the first hour, to the level of an occupied and conquered nation? Never!

He had just learned that the Americans had printed "Liberation Currency," American dollars denominated as French francs.

They were counterfeits, he told Churchill, and neither he nor his people would ever accept them. Nor were they going to accept an AMGOT. Although Churchill did not know it, de Gaulle had already set out carefully prepared plans to replace Vichy's government's structure with his own people as the liberation proceeded. The Allies could forget about those counterfeit American bills, he told Churchill, and he was not going to negotiate under what he considered intolerable pressure.

Churchill responded by repeating to de Gaulle a warning he had made two years earlier—don't try to force him to a choice, de Gaulle or Roosevelt, because his choice would inevitably be FDR.

"*Bien sur*," de Gaulle replied with a disdainful wave of his hand, "*bien sur*."

His meeting with Eisenhower went much better. The two men had an instinctive respect for each other. The American deferred to de Gaulle as an acting head of state, which his government did not do. De Gaulle had a good deal of esteem for Ike's capacities as a soldier/diplomat.

Eisenhower had come out of a meeting with his weathermen to brief de Gaulle on the coming invasion plans. The American's principal concern was securing law and order behind his lines as his troops advanced across France to the Ruhr. De Gaulle, he suspected, could give him that. He was much more inclined, therefore, to leave the management of France's domestic affairs to de Gaulle than Washington was.

When he'd finished his briefing, he explained the weather problems to de Gaulle and asked him for his advice.

His request pleased de Gaulle, who reflected a moment, then told Ike: Go ahead. The risks inherent in a postponement were worse than those posed by the weather.

Their meeting ended on a less engaging note. Eisenhower handed de Gaulle two texts. The first was the proclamation Eisenhower would make as Supreme Commander on D-Day morning announcing the invasion to the peoples of Occupied Europe.

The second, prepared by Eisenhower's staff, was the text of the speech the Allies wanted de Gaulle to broadcast to France on the morning of the invasion. What de Gaulle did not know, because he was completely unaware of the Allies' Fortitude deception scheme, was that the speech had been prepared to deliberately leave open the possibility of further Allied landings.

He accepted the texts with something less than good grace. No one, least of all an Anglo Saxon, wrote speeches for Charles de Gaulle.

The next day, he raised several objections to Eisenhower's text. Nowhere did the Supreme Commander refer to a French authority, to his Provisional Government, to his representatives in France.

Although de Gaulle didn't know it, Eisenhower had deliberately danced around instructions he had received from Roosevelt to make it clear in his speech that de Gaulle had no official status. In any event, Ike informed de Gaulle it was too late for him to modify his text; de Gaulle raised no objection.

For his own speech, however, it was a different matter. He threw away the Allies' text and wrote his own. The order in which the speeches were supposed to be read over the BBC was: the King of Norway, the queen of

Holland, the Grand Duchess of Luxembourg, the Prime Minister of Belgium, Eisenhower, and de Gaulle.

Quite predictably, de Gaulle was furious with that. France behind a nickel-and-dime duchy like Luxembourg? Never.

He would speak alone, on the evening of D-Day, and he would tell his compatriots exactly what he wanted them to hear: The orders given by his French government and by the French leaders that government had appointed were to be implicitly obeyed.

So much for the Allies AMGOT and its nominees.

De Gaulle's ultimate reply to his Anglo Saxon Allies came eight days after D-Day, on June 14, in the lovely Norman town of Bayeux. It was a *sous-prefecture*, the first administrative headquarters to be liberated.

On that morning, visiting France for the first time since 1940, de Gaulle went straight to the *sous-prefecture* where he was greeted by an M. Rochat, the Vichy *sous-préfet*. De Gaulle quizzed him on the food problems in the town, then ordered him to take down the portrait of Marshal Petain and replace it with a French flag.

That accomplished, de Gaulle dismissed Rochat and replaced him with his own *commissaire régional*, François Coulet.

Those were, of course, administrative gestures, important though largely symbolic acts. What mattered was what happened a few minutes later when de Gaulle stepped out onto the balcony of the *sous-prefecture*.

Virtually the entire population of the town was gathered in the street below. For fully five minutes, the crowd, nearly hysterical with joy, cheered the leader of the Free French. Later that afternoon, the same scene was repeated at Isigny and Grandcamp.

That was it. What his compatriots had given him in the streets of Bayeux, Isigny, and Grandcamp was something neither Churchill nor Roosevelt could deny him. It was the mandate of the French people. De Gaulle would receive its final consecration in the streets of Paris two months hence. But from that morning in Bayeux, it was clear that whether his Anglo Saxon Allies liked it or not, Charles de Gaulle was going to be the leader of a liberated France.

General Charles de Gaulle and General Charles-Emmanuel Mast, saluting the troops in Tunis, Tunisia, 1943.

9.

Halycon Plus Four

IT WAS NOON, Monday May 29, 1944, when a coded signal flashed out of General Dwight Eisenhower's forward battle headquarters at Southwick House, a large estate on the forward edge of a ridge of hills looking down on Portsmouth Harbor. "Halcyon plus Four" it said.

Inspired by the bird of ancient legend that could calm the unruly winds, those three words signaled to the Combined Chief of Staffs in London, to the White House and Pentagon in Washington, to the commanders of the air, sea, and land forces that would stage the invasion of Europe, that D-Day was set for a week hence, for Monday, June 5. The planning, the preparations, the rehearsals were over. All that Ike and his staff could do had been done. The machinery of the greatest military operation in history was beginning to turn. Everything hinged now on the imponderables, and particularly on that greatest imponderable of them all, the weather.

Yet Eisenhower could feel comfortable with his decision to send that coded cable. The weather for the last days had been perfect—warm, sunny, cloudless skies, little wind to trouble the waters of the Channel. Why wouldn't it remain that way?

It wouldn't because of mild disturbance a C-47 weather plane flying out of Newfoundland was picking up on the eastern tip of Canada at just about the time Eisenhower was releasing his cable. The weather off the North American seaboard was beginning to change. And the weather patterns that affect Europe generally move from west to east across the Atlantic Ocean.

Because the weather would be such a critical element in the invasion, Eisenhower had set up a special meteorological office next to his operations room. It was commanded by Group Captain John Stagg, the chief meteorologist of the RAF, seconded by U.S. Army Air Force Colonel D.N. Yates. They were linked to a pool of weather experts from the British Weather Service, the U.S. National Weather Bureau, the British Admiralty, and the RAF. To support their work, the weathermen were backed up by a chain of ships, land stations, and aircraft like the C-47 that had picked up the weather changes off the eastern coast of the North American continent. They ranged across the Atlantic through Greenland, Iceland, the Shetlands, and as far south as the Azores and Canary Islands.

At midday on Thursday June 1, just as the ships in the sea lochs of Scotland were weighing anchor, the situation worsened. What had been a suggestion of trouble 72 hours earlier had now crystallized into a distinct threat. The weather prospects for the three critical days of June 4, 5, and 6, Stagg had to tell the Supreme Commander, had suddenly become uncertain.

The next day, Friday June 2, Stagg would have to make his first critical presentation to Ike and his commanders. Studying his charts that morning, it was apparent to the RAF meteorologist that the weather had taken a major turn for the worse during the night. Long after the war, he would recall that the entire Atlantic Ocean seemed suddenly filled with a succession of depressions that morning. What was heading in from the North Atlantic was no longer a spell of bad weather—it was a major storm. Stagg was going to have to make a five-day forecast that evening for Eisenhower and his staff. To his dismay, no two of the great weather experts in his pool could agree about a forecast for as much as the next 24 hours, to say nothing of five days. The fate of the greatest operation of the Second World War was hanging in the balance and half a dozen weathermen couldn't make up their minds about a forecast on which its success or failure might depend.

Stagg, however, was taking no chances. The situation, he warned Eisenhower, was now "potentially full of menace." The storm front would move in on June 5 bringing with it low clouds and winds of at least Force Four or Five. Eisenhower decided to wait another 24 hours, until the evening of Saturday, June 3, before deciding whether or not to put the landings back 24 hours.

On that Saturday, the men and vehicles that would make the assault on the beaches of Normandy began to board the transports that would carry them to the Bay of the Seine. Shortly after sunset, the first of those transports formed into convoys and moved out to sea.

As Stagg entered the nine o'clock conference at Southwick House that evening, a British naval officer remarked, "Here comes six feet, two inches of gloom."

Gloom, indeed, is what Stagg was offering that night. The situation had worsened. He now saw winds of at least Force Five churning up the waters of the Channel. The cloud cover would be so low that parachute drops would be out of the question and aerial support for the assault waves problematic at best.

"Isn't there just a chance you might be a bit more optimistic tomorrow?" Eisenhower asked, almost begging for a glimmer of hope from his weatherman.

No, Stagg, told him, there wasn't.

And so, at 0415 on the morning of Sunday June 4, Eisenhower felt compelled to order, "Ripcord plus 24," the code phrase that would postpone the Normandy Invasion by 24 hours.

Holding the landings in abeyance for 24 hours was a staggeringly difficult task. Over 5000 ships, over two million men, military and civilian, were involved in one way or another in the gigantic enterprise. They had all now to be stopped in mid-stride, frozen in place. The ships bearing their troops desperately ill with seasickness would have to heave to or move in circles, praying a German reconnaissance flight, submarine, or E-boat wouldn't spot them. The miniature submarines that would mark the passage to the landing beaches would have to spend another 24 hours under water. Everything would have to go into a state of suspended animation on the unlikely hope the next 24 hours would bring a change in the weather.

Dawn brought the ultimate vindication to Eisenhower's worried weatherman. The storm had struck with even greater severity than he had predicted. Winds described by Eisenhower's historian as "near hurricane force" were ripping through the channel. To have attempted a landing on Monday June 5 would have certainly ended in an unmitigated disaster for the Allies.

The question which now faced Stagg and his pool of weather experts was whether that storm was going to continue and force another postponement of D-Day.

Except this time, the postponement would not be for 24 hours—it would have to be for 15 days, until June 20, the first date on which the landings could be attempted again. Studying his charts and the reports that had come in overnight from his weather stations, Stagg suddenly spotted a new and potentially dramatic development. One of the depressions out in the Atlantic just off Newfoundland had intensified and deepened during the night. That meant its progress across the ocean had slowed. That, in turn, meant there was a possibility there would be a gap between the cold front now storming through the channel and the arrival of the next depression.

Would that gap last long enough, would the weather during that brief interval be good enough, to allow the Allies to get ashore? If the answer to those questions was yes, there was every reason to hope the Germans, who lacked the long range weather stations the Allies had, would not have seen that break in the weather moving in. They would see only the storm now raging and conclude no landing was possible in such conditions. That little break in the weather just might give the Allied assault the one advantage no one had ever expected it to have—surprise.

While his meteorologists labored frantically with their forecast, Eisenhower waited and worried. He could have taken a bedroom suite in Southwick House, but he had chosen to live instead in what he called his "circus wagon," a truck-towed trailer. Late in the afternoon, he went for a walk through the estate's woods with Merrill "Red" Mueller, a correspondent of the American radio network, NBC. The correspondent did not dare intrude on the strained silence enveloping the usually cheerful Supreme Commander. Eisenhower, Mueller thought, seemed "bowed down with worry." It was as if each of the four stars he wore on his shoulders "weighed a ton."

Finally, at 2130, the decisive meeting was convened in the library of Southwick House, a large wood-paneled room, its walls lined by solid oak book cases. A conference table covered with a green baize cloth stood in the center of the room. The invasion's senior commanders were gathered around it, silent, worried men. All were in full uniform except for Montgomery who, as usual, wore corduroy slacks and a turtleneck sweater.

Ike entered on the stroke of nine-thirty. The famous Eisenhower grin was notably absent from his features that evening. As soon as he had taken his seat, Group Captain Stagg and his two senior deputies were summoned into the room.

"Gentlemen," Stagg said "there have been rapid and unexpected developments in the situation."

Outside, the storm continued to spatter the windows with rain and the gusting wind tore the fresh spring leaves off the larches ringing the great house. Yet there in the library, Stagg told the gathering of a "heaven sent hiatus" that would offer them a brief spell of reasonable weather. It would be far from good weather, but its conditions of wind, cloud, and sea would be enough—

barely—to meet the minimum standards their invasion demanded. The cloud cover would be high enough to allow an accurate bombardment by the Air Force and the naval guns off the beaches. The cloud cover over the areas in which the paratroopers would have to drop would be broken. Some moonlight would get through. Would it be enough for the pilots of the DC-3s to pick out their drop zones? That was impossible to predict. The seas would be running high, but not so high as to make the landing impossible.

It wasn't much those men were being offered—barely acceptable conditions for their landing and for only 24 hours at that.

Could their forecast be wrong? Eisenhower asked the weather men.

Of course it could, replied Stagg.

Eisenhower's Chief of Staff, General Walter Bedell Smith, urged they go ahead. How could they disembark their troops, thousands of whom had now been briefed on their D-Day targets, and hope to keep their plans secret for the two weeks they'd be ashore? The paratroopers would have a risky jump—but if they waited until June 19, their next available date, they'd have to jump without any moonlight at all.

The airmen, Air Chief Marshal Sir Arthur William

Tedder and Air Chief Marshal Sir Trafford Leigh-Mallory, both warned that air cover would be spotty.

Ike turned to Montgomery. "I would say 'go,'" Monty said.

It now came down to Eisenhower and Eisenhower alone. He sat motionless, his hands clasped before him on the table, wrapped, Bedell Smith thought, "in isolation and loneliness." Minutes ticked by while he weighed the possibilities. Then, he looked up, his face etched with strain.

"The question is just how long can you hang the operation on a limb and just let it hang there?" he asked. "I am quite positive we must give the order. I don't like it, but there it is."

Six hours later, at 0415 of Monday June 5, the men gathered again to confirm Eisenhower's decision. This time there was no discussion. General Eisenhower officially confirmed one of the most momentous decisions of that century. Relying on that most tenuous of predictions, a weatherman's forecast, he issued the final, irrevocable order for the invasion of Western Europe. Minutes later seven words in a coded cable: "Halcyon plus five finally and definitely confirmed" flashed his order to the soldiers, the sailors, and the airmen who would have to carry it out.

From that moment on there could be no turning back. In the berths and the moorings, the piers and ports, the coves and the inlets, from the Irish Sea, down the Welsh coast, in the Bristol Channel, and the Thames

Estuary, the invasion fleet began to move—5,000 ships and over a million men, the largest armada ever assembled, took to the waters. Fortune's wheel was now turning, its gyrations beyond man's control.

Eisenhower walked alone back to his trailer. Tucked into the breast pocket of his uniform jacket was a slip of paper. Nothing might measure better the unutterable solitude of a great captain at his hour of decision than the words on that paper. They were the communiqué Ike would release to the world's press if the invasion failed.

"The troops, the air and the navy did all that bravery and devotion to duty could do," it said. "If there is any blame or fault attached to the failure, it is mine alone."

Eisenhower's invasion headquarters were located at Southwick House, an estate overlooking Portsmouth Harbor, England.

10.

Rommel Heads Home

ROSE PETALS FLECKED the terrace like colored scraps of confetti left behind from a New Year's Eve celebration. Scraps of twigs littered its tiles and further on, where the green lawn began its descent to the chateau's garden, half a dozen branches ripped from the property's Linden trees bore mute testimony to the severity of the Channel storm that had punched its way through La Roche-Guyon in the hours before dawn. Standing at the double doors opening onto the terrace from his office, Field Marshal Erwin Rommel studied the scene with undisguised satisfaction.

Gusts of wind continued to send packets of leaves stripped from the Linden trees dancing past his windows. Clouds scudded down the horizon, low and menacing, bringing with them the promise that this was only a brief lull in the storm that had swept in from the Atlantic during the night. There would be little Allied fighter plane activity in the skies over France today. It was shortly before 0600, Monday, June 5, 1944.

Rommel went to the austere Renaissance desk on which Louis XIV's Minister of War had signed the revocation of the Edict of Nantes. It was his desk now and, as usual, it was bare of everything except for his copy of the morning report. That paper—uncharacteristically brief this stormy morning—summarized the activities in the 800-mile swath of land running from the dikes of Holland down to the rocky cliffs of Western Brittany that came under Rommel's purvey as Commander in Chief of Hitler's Army Group "B," the finest assortment of troops the Wehrmacht possessed in the springtime of 1944.

He picked up his field telephone and, under the gaze of the 17th century Duke Francois VI de la Rochefoucauld, author of the famous "Maxims" and forbearer of the chateau's current owner, Rommel placed a call to Army Group "B"'s chief meteorologist, Major Ernst Winkler. Winkler's headquarters were in a requisitioned seaside residence, the Villa Les Sapioles, at Wimereux on the Channel coast just outside the city of Boulogne.

The weather could hardly be worse, Winkler informed Rommel. From his window he could look down on surf a meter-and-a-half high, driven by Force Six winds, crashing onto the beach. The landing craft that could get troops safely onto the shore in a sea like that was yet to be made.

Winkler's visual observation confirmed the judgement laid down in Rommel's morning report by the Luftwaffe's chief meteorologist in Paris, Colonel Professor Walter Strobe. The next 48 hours, Strobe predicted, would bring the French Channel seacoast nothing but increased cloudiness, high winds and rain. The cloud base inland from the Channel coast would, he estimated, range between 900 and 1800 feet, a ceiling much too low to permit a paratroop landing. Clearly, the Allies were not going to launch their invasion of the Continent in weather like that. May had been an idyllic month of blue skies, warm weather, and little wind—perfect invasion weather. And yet the Allies had not come.

Their failure to do so had sharpened a growing conviction among the German command in the west that the Allies weren't finished with their invasion preparations quite yet, that they had decided to launch their assault in coordination with the opening of the Russians' summer offensive, expected in the last 10 days of June when the Polish countryside had finally dried out after the nation's traditionally late thaws.

Rommel had every reason to be well satisfied with the weather reports he received that June morning some 60 years ago.

Outside, in front of the chateau's formal entrance, Rommel's black open Horch waited. His Aide-de-Camp, Captain Helmuth Lang, had already placed a lunch basket of sandwiches, a flask of consommé, and a flask of tea in the car beside the driver's seat. For weeks, Lang and Rommel had begun their days by climbing into that car shortly after dawn, off to inspect another outpost in the chain of Atlantic fortifications under Rommel's command. Rommel was leaving his headquarters at La Roche-Guyon as usual that morning, but it was not to inspect another of his Atlantic fortifications.

The Field Marshal was going home. He was leaving for his residence in the town of Herrlingen in the province of Ulm.

The legend has grown up over the years that the reason Rommel was leaving that day was so that he could be at home to celebrate the birthday of his wife, Marie Lucie, on Tuesday, June 6.

That legend is quite inexact. It is true that Rommel was planning to spend June 6 with his wife, but that pleasure was incidental to the real reason for his trip. That reason was a meeting he had scheduled for the next day, Wednesday, June 7, at the Berghof with Adolf Hitler and, above all, the request he was determined to press on Hitler at their meeting.

He was going to ask Hitler to release to him immediately two further Panzer divisions, the 2nd SS stationed in Toulouse and the 9th Panzer in Avignon. In their present locations, neither of those divisions was going to be of any use in the coming invasion. It was time to get them into positions where they could intervene in the early hours of an Allied attack.

Rommel knew precisely what those positions should be. He was going to bring those divisions to Normandy. He wanted them stationed south and west of Caen where they could intervene in the first 24 hours of a landing at the base of the Cotentin Peninsula—on the very beaches on which the Allies would soon becoming ashore. He was confident he would get Hitler's agreement to the transfer of those divisions. He was, after all, the Fuhrer's favorite Field Marshal. But much more important, since the first of May, Normandy had been at the center of Hitler's—and hence—Rommel's concerns.

On May 1, Hitler's Oberkommando der Wehrmacht headquarters (OKW or Supreme Command of the Armed Forces) had telephoned the Chateau de La Roche-Guyon in Rommel's absence and asked his Chief of Staff, General Hans Speidel, if he was certain the forces currently assigned to Normandy could defeat an invasion there. The following day, without even waiting for Speidel's answer, Hitler ordered the 91st Luftwaffe Airborne Division and several armoured and anti-tank battalions as reinforcements to Normandy.

Barely a week later, an urgent telex from Hitler's headquarters informed Rommel that the invasion was to be expected "in the middle of May...point of concentration: first and foremost, Normandy."

Rommel was not convinced. On the evening of May 15th he exercised his privilege as a Field Marshal and picked up the telephone, which linked him directly to Hitler's headquarters. Why, he asked General Alfred Jodl, was the Fuhrer focusing so much attention on Normandy?

The Fuhrer, Hitler's Chief of Staff informed Rommel, had "certain information" that Normandy and the port of Cherbourg would be the first objective of the Allies' landing. Where did that information come from? Was it a manifestation of Hitler's famous intuition? Was it a startlingly precise report from an Abwehr agent somewhere in the world?

There is nothing in the German archives to explain it. Nor did any of Hitler's close associates give an explanation for it in their interrogations after the war. Yet the fact is there—for whatever reason, Hitler had come up with an uncannily accurate assessment of the Allies' intentions by the middle of May, 1944.

His concern had prompted Rommel to make another inspection of the Cotentin Peninsula. On Wednesday, May 17, with his naval aide, Admiral Friederich Oskar Ruge beside him, he stood on the desolate strip of sand that would soon become Utah Beach. For a long time, Ruge would one day recall, Rommel stared out at the flat gray sea as if he was envisioning the invasion fleet that would soon rise upon its waters.

"So," he said to the sailor, "this is where you think they'll land."

It was, Ruge told him, because as a sailor he knew that the waters before them were sheltered by the Cotentin land mass from the Channel's prevailing winds.

The mariner's wisdom was not enough to convince the soldier, however.

"No," Rommel told Ruge finally, "they will come where the crossing is shortest, where their fighter planes will be closest to their bases."

His inspection did, however, lead Rommel to make one critical decision, the decision behind his departure for Herrlingen and Berchtesgaden this stormy morning. He would get those two additional Panzer divisions from Hitler in his meeting with the dictator on Wednesday, he was confident of that. By June 20 he would have them marshaled behind those beaches soon to be known as Sword, Gold, Juno, Omaha, and Utah, their fuel tanks topped up, their munitions racks full, their engines warm, their crews ready. Once he had those Panzers in place, no Allied landing, he was sure, would get a foothold on those Norman beaches. Two weeks was all he needed. Two weeks and he would have made the last corner of the Atlantic Wall impregnable.

He issued a few last-minute orders—a missive to Luftwaffe headquarters in Paris requesting stepped-up aerial surveillance of the Channel ports on both sides of the Thames as soon as the skies cleared, a suggestion to his Chief of Staff General Hans Speidel that in view of the weather, they stand down their troops. The men, he noted, could use a rest after a month of constant invasion alerts. Then, with a last reassuring look at the stormy sky, he set out for his waiting car.

Once Rommel had told a group of the soldiers under his command: "Do not look for the enemy by daylight when the sun is shining. They will come at night in cloud and storm."

He was right. That was exactly how they were coming. And he may very well have been right, too, in thinking no Allied landing could succeed in Normandy once he had his two Panzer divisions in place.

But, because of the courageous decision made a few hours earlier by a Kansas farmer to maintain his D-Day landings despite the weather, the gods of war were not going to give the Desert Fox the two weeks he needed to get them there.

Rommel got into the back seat of the Horch beside his aide Captain Lang. His operations officer was in front beside the driver, Daniel.

"*Mach schnell,*" Rommel ordered Daniel. The car started up the alley of Linden trees lining the drive of the chateau. As it did, far across the Channel, in the Wash and the Irish Sea, the ships of the great armada that would deliver the invaders to those beaches on which Rommel had vowed to defeat them were already moving into their assembly areas.

As he had gotten into the the Horch, Rommel had placed a box on the seat beside him. It contained a pair of gray shoes the Field Marshal had bought in Paris a few days before as a birthday present for his wife—shoes his foes would later claim had cost Germany the war.

Troops and crewmen aboard a Coast Guard manned LCVP as it approaches a Normandy beach on D-Day, June 6, 1944.

11.

Verlaine's
Sobbing Violins

IT WAS A NIGHTLY ritual, a ritual as important for a member of the French Resistance as reciting his daily breviary was for a parish priest. Each evening during that anxious springtime of 1944, in Paris, Rennes and Calais, Lille, Lyons, and Rouen, the men and women of the Resistance huddled beside their radio sets listening to the forbidden broadcasts of the BBC. Their ears were alerted for the long list of *messages personnels* following the news, waiting for a phrase that might send them into the night to fight, perhaps to die, in support of an Allied assault on their occupied nation.

What a body of lore has grown up around those messages! What memories the sound of that disembodied voice coming over the air can still stir today among those men and women who once listened for those messages.

The idea for using them as a way to alert a Resistance network for action goes all the way back to

1942, long before anyone was seriously contemplating an invasion. The idea was simple. A Resistance network in the field would be given two key phrases. If the first of the two phrases, the alert phrase, was broadcast on either the first or the fifteenth of a month, it would mean the network to which it had been assigned was placed on alert for the next 15 days. Its members would have to listen every night for the second action, part of the phrase. If it didn't come during those 15 days, then the alert was canceled. But if it did come, it would mean an attack was going to take place in 48 hours and the network was to proceed immediately with its pre-assigned sabotage missions.

One of those alert/action phrases, a couplet from Paul Verlaine's *"Chanson d'Automne"* *("Autumn Song")*— *"Les sanglots longs des violons de l'automne....blessent mon coeur d'une langueur monotone"* (The long sobs of autumn's violins wound my heart with a monotonous languor)— was now to enter into the legends of the Normandy Landings, and for all the wrong reasons.

Here, perhaps for the first time in its full detail, is the story behind those two lines of poetry and how they came to be broadcast by the Allies and intercepted by the Germans. The two Verlaine lines were first sent into Occupied France as alert/action messages not in 1944, but in 1943. They had nothing whatsoever to do with the Normandy Invasion.

They were given to the three members of a network belonging to the British-run Special Operations Executive (SOE), François Garel, Marcel Fox, and Marcel Rousset. No Allied Invasion of Europe was contemplated for 1943—so why were those three men given alert/action messages?

Their network, called Butler, had links to a much larger SOE organization based in Paris and called Prosper.

The Prosper network, however, had been penetrated by the Gestapo operating out of the Avenue Foch. Many of its agents were under German surveillance as early as the late spring of 1943. MI6 in London, the Secret Intelligence Service, knew that the organization had been penetrated. They did not communicate that information, however, to the leadership of the SOE's French Section. Ignorant, therefore, of what had happened, the SOE had no reason to warn its agents inside France that they risked arrest.

Why were they not told? The Allies' deception plan for the summer of 1943, called "Starkey," was designed to convince the Germans that the Allies would land in France in September, 1943 and thus lead the Germans to hold a maximum number of divisions in France during the summer, well away from the Eastern Front and the sorely pressed Russians. It is now quite clear that once it had become evident that the Prosper network had been penetrated, its agents in the field were cynically used to further the aims of that 1943 deception plan rather than given information that would have saved them from German arrest.

Prosper's leader, Francis Suthill, was called to London and given a secret briefing by Churchill himself. Suthill would later tell his Resistance colleagues in Paris the Prime Minister had intimated to him that the invasion would come in the fall.

The SOE was instructed to send its agents into the field that spring and summer with alert and action messages—just in case an invasion should come. Most of those alert/action messages went to people associated with the penetrated Prosper network. It was soon being whispered throughout the network that the invasion was coming in the fall and that the organization would have a vital role to play in supporting it.

What in fact happened was that the Gestapo began to round up the network's members in a series of arrests over the summer. Garel, Fox, and Rousset were arrested by the Gestapo in Paris on September 7, 1943 in what they thought was a safe house but had been betrayed to the Gestapo by one of the agents swept up in the arrests of Prosper members and its affiliated networks.

The Gestapo officers immediately turned their not altogether tender attentions on the radio operator, Rousset. Rousset told them that he transmitted to London in English for Garel and in French for Fox. In fact, the opposite was true. He transmitted in French for Garel and English for Fox. Assuming London would realize he was transmitting under German control if he reversed his procedure, he agreed to send a message to London for the Gestapo. It would be from Garel. It would ask for money. And it would be in English.

In an act of either total cynicism or unbelievable stupidity, London answered by asking him why he had switched his modus operandi. Thus betrayed, Rousset gave the Gestapo, among other things, his alert/action messages from the Verlaine couplet. Either Fox or Garel confirmed his information in a separate interrogation.

The information was sent for analysis to Colonel Oskar Reille, head of the Abwehr's Section IIIF at the Hotel Lutetia.

Reille understood the significance of the messages and the meaning that was to be attached to them perfectly. On October 14, 1943, Reille circulated the two lines from the poem in ABW 4508/43 together with an accurate explanation of how the timing of each line worked and what its broadcast would mean.

What Reille didn't realize, however, was that the two lines *had already been broadcast over the BBC*—some time in the weeks immediately following the arrest of Fox, Garel, and Rousset, presumably once London had realized the three had been captured by the Germans.

One senior German officer was not impressed by Reille's intelligence coup, Field Marshal Gerd von Rundstedt, the Commander in Chief in the West. It was October, he pointed out. There was no chance that the Allies would attempt a landing in the middle of winter. Their earliest landing date would be late April. Were they going to be stupid enough to send these alert/action messages into the field six or seven months before their landings and run the risk that the men and women who had those messages might be captured and reveal them under torture?

Of course they weren't, the old Field Marshal said, adding a phrase that would go down in history: "The Allies aren't going to announce they're coming over the BBC."

And indeed, beginning in February 1944, a systematic effort was taken to cancel all the old alert/action messages which had been sent out and to replace them with an entirely new set of messages. Wherever possible, the leader of a network was allowed to choose his own messages. After all, it was he who would have to remember them as the landings approached.

At the Baker Street offices of the SOE in London, a very attractive red-headed Canadian girl had the responsibility of keeping track of each set of messages which were being been sent into the field. She had to record which network had been assigned which phrases, making sure there was no duplication in the messages and that none of the outmoded 1943 messages were assigned to anybody.

In March 1944, Philippe de Vomécourt, head of a SOE network in Loire–et-Cher, called Ventriloquist, was in London. Before heading back into the field, he was asked to choose his alert/action messages. He picked the two first lines of one of his favorite poems, Verlaine's "Chanson d'Automne." The Canadian lady who was supposed to scrutinize all the messages going out into the field did not catch the fact that the couplet had already been employed in 1943 and might, therefore, be compromised. Her error seems to be nothing more sinister than a sheer administrative blunder. As a result, de Vomécourt's messages were erroneously entered into the SOE's message book.

As the invasion approached, the Allies, knowing the Germans followed the flow of the *messages personnels* attentively, began to use them as a way of setting off false alarms among the listening Germans. One day 350 messages would be broadcast. The German troops in France would be put on alert. Three days later, no messages would be broadcast. The troops would go back on alert.

Von Rundstedt saw it all as the psychological ploy it was, a tactic to fray German nerves and wear out his troops with false alerts. Forget the messages, he ordered his staff.

Reille, however, was sure that the *sanglots* of those violins of M. Verlaine were going to give him the secret of the invasion. And indeed, on June 1, Sergeant Walter Reichling at the 15th Army Communications Reconnaissance Post, in a concrete bunker in Tourcoing, heard the first part of the message not once, but three times.

Reille went into a state of high frenzy. He ordered the Tourcoing listening post to be particularly alert in the days ahead.

At 2115 on the night of Monday, June 5, London broadcast the second line of the poem for de Vomécourt and his Ventriloquist network. Reille was working at his desk at the Hotel Lutetia when a duty sergeant burst into his office with the news. He ordered a car from the motor pool and sped off for von Rundstedt's Saint Germain-en-Laye headquarters. Racing through Paris' deserted streets, he thought of how important the information he carried was. He held in his hands, he told himself, "Germany's last chance."

And he was not far from wrong. For all the wrong reasons, Reille did, indeed, have in his hands the secret that the invasion was coming—a full nine-and-a-half hours before the assault waves would hit the shore, almost four hours before the first paratroops would tumble out of the night skies.

Von Rundstedt's intelligence officer, Colonel Wilhelm Meyer-Detring, was in Berlin on leave. Reille gave his precious information to Detring's assistant, a Major Brink. Brink promised him he would take the information to von Rundstedt's Operations Officer, Major General Bodo Zimmermann, immediately.

Reille returned to the Lutetia exultant. He ordered Monsieur Charles, the hotel's sommelier, to bring him the best bottle of champagne left in his cave so he could celebrate his triumph. He had done it; he had pierced the secret of the invasion. He had saved Germany from the disaster that had been about to strike her.

He had done nothing of the sort.

At Saint Germain-en-Laye, Zimmermann didn't even bother to show Reille's great scoop to von Rundstedt. It could wait until morning. All Zimmermann had to do was look at the storm beating on his window to know the message was just another of the Allies' psychological ploys. Let the troops sleep soundly for once, he decided.

Do not order an alert, he advised Rommel's headquarters. One of Rommel's two armies, the 15th in the Pas-de-Calais, had already been alerted. Its commander, General Hans von Salmuth, while playing bridge with his officers, had been informed that the second half of the message had come in directly by Tourcoing.

"I'm too old a bunny to get excited about this," he remarked, but told an aide to put the troops on alert anyway. Then he went back to his game.

That was the sum result of Reille's great triumph. The wrong army got put on alert. The one on which the invasion was about to fall continued to sleep the night away.

But there was another warning that the invasion fleet was coming, this one being deliberately passed to the Germans by the Allies. The master double agent, the Spaniard Juan Garcia, code named "Garbo," had been authorized, by General Eisenhower himself, to tell his Abwehr controllers in Madrid the Allies were coming at 0300—three-and-a-half hours before the first wave landed, but just too late to be of any use to the Germans. The report, however, was designed to make Garbo appear, in German eyes, as the spy of the century.

Garbo, his British Control Officer Tommy Harris, and an officer from Eisenhower's staff, had a festive dinner at Harris' home celebrating their coming triumph with Harris' 1934 Château Ausone.

Their story was a simple modification of the report they had sent Madrid in May. Number Four, one of Garbo's wholly imaginary sub-agents working in the camp housing the 3rd Canadian Infantry Division, a unit soon to land on Juno Beach, had informed the Spaniard that the Canadians had once again been issued cold rations, life jackets, and vomit bags and left camp.

Except this time, their place had been taken by a new American division. There could be no doubt—the invasion was on.

Precisely at 0300, Garbo's radio operator called up Madrid to pass the Germans that precious bit of information.

Madrid didn't answer. For two hours the usually vigilant Abwehr signalman in Madrid was silent. Here the Allies were desperate to lay their great secret in his hands and the wretched man was probably out chasing flamenco dancers in a Madrid cabaret.

Finally, at 0500, Garbo's controller received permission from Eisenhower's headquarters to add considerable additional information to his message.

It would make his text a spymaster's dream—but would it be enough to make Garbo appear so infallible in German eyes that they would be ready to swallow the enormous lie he would pass them 48 hours hence?

AUTUMN SONG
By Paul Verlaine

The long sobs
of autumn's
violins
wound my heart
with a monotonous
languor.

Suffocating
and pallid, when
the clock strikes,
I remember
the days long past
and I weep.

And I set off
in the rough wind
that carries me
hither and thither
like a dead
leaf.

12.

A Flag for Sainte-Mère-Église

THE LONG-AWAITED invasion of Western Europe began, not to the thunder of naval gunfire or the crash of exploding bombs, but in a silence broken only by the moaning of the wind. As midnight on June 5 ticked past, there was not a single German patrol boat prowling the waters of the Channel. All naval activity had been stood down by Admiral Theodor Kranke, the German Naval Commander in the West. The seas, he had declared, were running too high to permit a landing. Those few planes of the Luftwaffe available for aerial reconnaissance missions were grounded because of the weather. Rommel, the man who had vowed to defeat the Allies at the water's edge, was sound asleep at his home in Herrlingen. General Fritz Bayerlein, commander of the crack Panzer Lehr Division, was asleep in the arms of his mistress in Paris.

Indeed, so many senior German officers were absent from their posts that night, Hitler's headquarters would order an investigation—not that the Fuhrer himself had been notably alert either. He had listened to classical music in the Berghof, his home in the Obersalzberg of the Bavarian Alps, with his mistress Eva Braun before taking his usual sleeping potion and retiring just before 0200.

Across the Channel, the Allied commanders were haunted by fear and anxiety. "It may well be the most ghastly disaster of the whole war," Field Marshal Sir Alan Brooke, Chief of the Imperial General Staff, wrote in his diary that night. "I wish to God it were safely over."

"Tonight is the worst of the war," recorded General Sir Hastings Ismay, Winston Churchill's Chief of Staff. Churchill spent the night in his underground command post at Storey's Gate in London, drinking brandy and brooding on what the next 72 hours might bring. Colonel John Bevan, the man responsible for putting Plan Fortitude, the scheme to deceive the Germans on the Allies' real intentions, walked the streets of London, chain-smoking his Players cigarettes, worrying if his scheme had any prospect of success.

General Dwight Eisenhower, on whose shoulders the whole immense operation rested, visited with the embarking paratroopers of the U.S. 82nd and 101st Airborne Divisions. Watching those men climb into their DC-3s, their faces blackened, their heads shaved Apache style; he knew it was they who risked paying a terrible price for his decision to go ahead with the invasion.

It was just minutes after midnight when the first of the 9,200 Allied aircraft that would fill the skies this day, a pair of Stirling bombers of the RAF, cleared British airspace and headed across the Channel for the Cherbourg peninsula. Each dropped a pair of three-man teams, then continued inland to drop their real cargos, the first Allied "soldiers" to land in number as part of the invasion.

They were not fighting troops at all, but 200 rubber dummies, "Rupert" dolls with parachutes that opened and firecrackers that exploded in mid-air like gunfire. Their purpose was to draw the German defenders inland away from what would be the drop zones of the real airborne troops coming 90 minutes later.

As the Germans were beginning to react to their lure, RAF Halifaxes were skimming the Brittany peninsula, dropping the first sticks of the 4th SAS, French paratroopers plunging into Brittany to provide cadres for the Breton Resistance in the coming struggle. As one stick stumbled to the ground outside Vannes, a burst of automatic weapons fire cut into their ranks. One of their number, a corporal named Emile Bouétard, tumbled dead to the ground. With sad appropriateness, a French soldier had become the first Allied casualty in the battle for France.

(A stick consists of paratroopers who jump from the door of an aircraft during a run over a drop zone. Because of mission requirements and the size of the plane used for a drop, the number of paratroopers in a stick is a highly variable number. For D-Day, most sticks would have numbered around 18-20 paratroopers.)

As he fell, all across France but most particularly through the invasion area, the men and women of the Resistance began to put Plan Violet, the sabotage of German telecommunications, into effect. They cut overhead telephone lines, dug up and spiked underground cables, blew up repeater stations, sabotaged central switchboards.

Just after 0015 the first pathfinders of the three airborne divisions that would drop into Normandy tumbled out of their aircraft into the French night. All veterans of combat landings, all were volunteers. The Americans had been trained by Brigadier General James "Jumping Jim" Gavin. Gavin had warned them they would have only one friend when they hit the ground—God.

Their orders were to avoid the Germans and combat at all cost. They were to have one concern only—to get to the areas they were supposed to mark out as drop zones as fast as they could, then lay down their fluorescent panels and set in place the special light and radio beams that would guide the oncoming air trains to their destination.

They would have barely an hour to do their job and success, therefore, depended on the pathfinders getting an accurate drop.

Few did. Only a third of the American pathfinders dropped onto their targets. Some came down miles away, in unfamiliar territory with no visible landmarks to point them toward their goal, nothing besides a compass and their instincts to guide their steps.

The majority of the British pathfinders had a better and more accurate drop, due probably to the greater skill and experience of the RAF pilots bringing them in. Their key objective was to seize a pair of bridges crossing two parallel waterways, the Caen Canal and the Orne River below Caen between the villages of Ranville and Benouville. Those bridges had to be seized and held to prevent German armour from using them to drive into the flank of the landings on Sword Beach.

And they had to be captured intact so the Allies could use them later to expand their beachhead.

To do it required speed, surprise, and a daring strategy: the British would assault the bridges' defenders by landing six gliders right at the foot of the bridges themselves. One hundred and fifty men were in the assault party led by Major John Howard. Cast off by their tow bombers at 5,000 feet and five miles out to sea, the gliders' pilots brought their bat-like craft swooping out of the skies and onto the bridge approaches with perfect accuracy. For most of the Germans, the first indication they were under attack came from the crashing and scraping of the gliders plowing to a halt right in front of their positions. Stunned by the surprise and the boldness of the Allies' attack, the Germans were overwhelmed in less than 15 minutes. It was D-Day's first, outstanding success.

The airborne assault, due to start coming in an hour after the pathfinders had dropped, would be considerably less successful.

Everything about the Normandy Landings would go into the history books surrounded by superlatives—the biggest this the largest that—and, indeed, quite accurately. Thus it was with the airborne assault—it was the largest airborne invasion ever attempted before or after D-Day. Eighteen thousand men from three Allied divisions, the 82nd and 101st American, the 6th British, plus three enormous glider trains, were about to descend on Normandy.

However, the bad weather and poor visibility, the anti-aircraft fire, the fact so many of the pathfinders had been dropped so far from the zones they were supposed to mark out, all contributed to drops that were in some cases close to disastrous. For the American divisions, part of the difficulties came from DC-3 pilots who'd had no experience in combat flying. Some panicked at anti-aircraft fire, lost their bearings and wandered far off course in an effort to avoid the ground fire. Some pilots had to be forced to fly on to their drop zones at gunpoint.

The 101st Airborne was dropped over an area of 400 square miles. Within an hour, the division had lost 60 percent of its equipment and 2000 men. Rommel's flooded fields took an appalling toll. Men weighted down by heavy packs, weapons, and ammunition drowned in the mud and slime of those flooded fields before they could even get out of the parachute harnesses.

The 82nd's drop was, if anything, even less successful. Only one of its planes dropped its troops exactly where they were supposed to land. At Ste-Mère-Église, a raging fire, probably set off by a stray incendiary bomb, lit up the night sky and served as an unwanted beacon to the oncoming DC-3s. Perhaps 50, 82nd troopers dropped into the center of the town, some into the blaze itself. One, Private John Steele, hung suspended from the church steeple for two hours before the Germans cut him down and took him prisoner.

All through the Norman night, fields and hedgerows echoed to the unfamiliar sound of crickets chirping. They came from metal snappers, like children's toys, which each of the Americans were issued in England as a way of identifying each other—one snap would be answered by a double snap as a recognition signal.

Gradually, men began to gather in small groups and move to their objectives. Of first importance was securing the fields on which the glider trains bringing in reinforcements of men, material, and light artillery pieces were due to land two hours after the parachute drops.

The 101st's glider landings, unlike the division's

drop, were remarkably successful. Only a handful of the incoming gliders were lost. Thanks to the equipment they pulled from the wreckage of the gliders, the few troopers who'd gotten to their landing zones could begin to assault the division's objectives.

Rommel had turned the strip of land behind what was going to become Utah Beach into a 12-mile square lake, leaving the beach an isolated island between the sea and his lake. Five causeways crossed over the flooded areas, all held by well dug-in German troops. The 101st would have to seize those causeways during the night. Otherwise, the men landing on Utah beach would be bottled up on the sands, unable to move inland.

The 82nd's glider landings were less successful. Only a half of the division's gliders got to the ground where they were supposed to. Nonetheless, Lt. Col. Edward C. Krause of the 505th Regiment led his men onto their first objective, the crossroads town of Ste-Mère-Église. After the shock of the first accidental drops into the village, the Germans had largely withdrawn. The town was liberated by 0430.

Krause went to the town hall and pulled an American flag from his knapsack. The flag had flown over Naples after the city's capture by the regiment in 1943. Proudly, Krause hauled it into the dawn sky over the first commune in France to be liberated.

On the eastern flank of the invasion area, the British airborne landings were more successful, although there too some 6th Airborne units were scattered widely over the countryside. Once again, Rommel's flooded fields proved to be the deadliest enemy that night. Dozens of young men drowned struggling to get out of the swamps and marshes of the wastelands caused by the flooding of the Dives River.

For the British paratroopers, the rallying sound was not the chirp of a cricket but the baleful bleat of the horn used to summon gentlemen riders in pursuit of a fleeing fox. The 6th had five-and-a-half hours to form up and secure the invasion's left flank by helping to hold the twin bridges over the Orne and destroying five lesser bridges over the Dives.

One unit, Lt. Col. Terence Otway's 9th Battalion, had the most difficult assignment of the night. They had to neutralize the four guns installed in a German coastal artillery battery at Merville, guns the Allies believed would devastate the troops landing on Sword Beach if they were not put out of action.

The position was surrounded by defenses in depth: mine fields, coils of barbed wire, more mine fields, machine gun emplacements, and finally the battery itself, defended by 200 men.

Initially the plan called for two gliders to land right on the roof of the battery as Otway's men launched their attack. They couldn't, however, because Otway had lost in his drop the radio he needed to inform the gliders he was ready to attack. Without his message, the gliders wouldn't cast off from their tow planes.

So Otway had to lead his 150 men in their assault unaided. Sappers cleared a path through the mines. Bangalore torpedoes tore a hole in the wire. Otway's men did the rest. Only 22 Germans survived their assault. He lost 70 men. But the guns were spiked and Otway was able to fire off a yellow victory flare informing the fleet offshore that the battery had been disabled.

General Sir Hastings Lionel Ismay, Winston Churchill's Chief of Staff

It was, with the U.S. Rangers assault on the cliffs of the Pointe du Hoc, the outstanding feat of arms of D-Day. It was also, along with the action at the Pointe du Hoc, to be the most futile. The 75mm guns the battery enclosed couldn't have reached Sword Beach anyway.

13.

The Frenchmen of the SAS

THE SAS—SPECIAL Action Service. Pronounce the name of that elite fighting force today, and what image comes to mind? Surely that of British soldiers, faces blackened, landing their rubber boats behind the Argentine lines in the Falklands War or dropping into the Iraqi desert to spot missile sites in the Gulf wars.

Few people would be likely to associate French troops with that organization, certainly the most intensely trained, highly motivated organization of its kind in the world.

Yet the fact is that when the first full brigade of that legendary force was established in advance of the D-Day Invasion during the winter of 1944, half of its 800-man complement, two of its four companies, were French. Those 400 Frenchmen in that distinguished company played an absolutely critical and little-known role in the Normandy Invasion and the liberation of their nation.

Their company had been one of the very first Free French fighting units set up by General de Gaulle after his arrival in London in June, 1940. He wanted to create an elite strike force—a force that would be capable of carrying out military missions inside Occupied France while in uniform. It would be his way of reminding both the German occupiers and their French subjects that a French Army still existed, that its soldiers were still carrying on the struggle against the Nazi regime.

In March 1941, the company went into action for the first time. Captain Georges Berger and four men dropped into Brittany in uniform near Vannes. The Luftwaffe had stationed there an elite group of pilots who were playing an essential role in the aerial bombardment of England. They flew to the targets ahead of the bombers and illuminated them with flares so the oncoming bomber force couldn't miss their assignment.

The pilots were billeted in a hotel in Vannes and taken in the evening by bus to their airfield. Berger's assignment was to ambush the bus and kill the pilots.

By the time of their drop, however, the pilots had been moved to barracks on the airbase at Elven. The mission was aborted. The next assignment, destroying an electric power plant outside Bordeaux that provided power to a submarine pen, was carried out without a hitch.

At that point General de Gaulle decided he wanted his elite band of soldiers to fight as a unit on the battlefield. The company was flown to the Middle East to participate in the campaign against the Vichy regime in Syria and Lebanon.

When the Middle East campaign ended, Berger recruited replacements in Beirut and flew the newcomers to Egypt for parachute training. There he met the legendary Colonel David Stirling, founding father of the SAS. Stirling had just assembled the forerunner of the SAS, the Long Range Desert Penetration Group. Its job had been to do on the ground what the RAF couldn't do in the air—destroy the Luftwaffe (air fleet) supporting Rommel's Afrika Corps.

So successful had Stirling's first forays behind the German lines been that he'd been authorized to double his force.

But where was he going to find the kind of highly trained and motivated men he needed?

Berger and his 100 Free French Paratroopers looked ideal to Stirling. Berger and his men were all for it. But there was a problem. De Gaulle was having one of his periodic clashes with the English. He had vowed never to let a Frenchman of his serve under British superiors again.

Still, Stirling went to see the General in Beirut. He presented his case as forcefully as he could. De Gaulle listened sympathetically. He was well aware of Stirling's work and reputation. Still, agreeing to Stirling's plea was out of the question as far as he was concerned.

As he accompanied his crestfallen caller to the door, Stirling remarked that it was the first time in his life as a stubborn Scot that he had failed to achieve what he'd set out to do.

"A Scot?" said de Gaulle. "Why didn't you say so? Come back in."

And so, in memory of the old French alliance with Mary Queen of Scots, Stirling got his 100 Free French paras.

The French contingent participated in a series of highly successful assaults on Luftwaffe bases that resulted in the destruction of well over 50 German aircraft on the ground. Captain Berger was taken prisoner in one of those operations against Crete in June 1942.

Once Rommel's Afrika Korps had been defeated, the SAS Brigade was brought back to England for the run-up to the invasion. Its mission, with no more Luftwaffe planes to blow up on the ground, was now redefined. They would train at night and fight at night. They would fight as small groups in pursuit of special objectives and be trained to fight as independent units.

The SAS was authorized to become something close in strength to the brigade they had been pretending to be—800 men of whom 400 were to be French, a tribute to the fighting capacity displayed by the 100 men of the original Free French Squadron.

For the English and the French squadrons, the recruiting process was strict; the training in the wilds of Scotland extremely difficult. Among the first of the new recruits into the French ranks was a 29-year-old lieutenant named Pierre Marienne. Born in Morocco, Marienne had been captured by the Vichy authorities while trying to escape to Gibraltar so he could join de Gaulle. He was brought back to Casablanca for trial where he set the courtroom into an uproar with his defiant attitude towards the judges trying him.

He shouted "Vive De Gaulle" as a standard way of concluding each of his answers to the court, denied the jurisdiction and the legality of his judges and captors, whom he labeled as traitors.

Furious, the court decided to make an example of Marienne and sentenced him to death. He was saved from the firing squad by the Allied landings in North Africa. Once free, he rushed to England to join de Gaulle's forces, then enlisted in the ranks of the SAS.

At the time of the Normandy landings, there were 150,000 German troops in Brittany. It was vital to keep them there, to prevent them from flowing out of the peninsula to reinforce the Germans' defenders in Normandy.

That was the task given to the SAS—their 800 men were to prevent or at least hinder the movement of 150,000 Germans. Furthermore, the British Secret

Intelligence Service and the Gaullist BCRA *(Bureau Central de Renseignements et d'Action)*—the Gaullist intelligence service first established in London—warned that the Breton Resistance had been badly hit by the Gestapo in April and the SAS troopers would have to make their jumps blind.

The first drops were to be made by four sticks of nine men each. Their job was to prepare the way for the bulk of the SAS forces that would follow them by marking out the drop zones on which they would land. They would be close to what would become two SAS bases, Sam West on the northern side of the peninsula and Dickson near Morbihan.

Marienne and Lieutenant Henri Desplantes—an aeronautical engineer who would become the designer of the Mirage fighter plane—volunteered to lead the first sticks.

Twenty-four hours before the drop, each man in the first stick was given a plastic sack into which he could put his personal mementos and letters to friends. They would get their sacks back if and when they returned alive.

Marienne had a personal emblem. It was a French flag with the Cross of Lorraine embroidered on its white slash. Under the cross were the words *"Vaincre ou Mourir."* Marienne had crossed out the word *"ou/*or." He had replaced it with *"et/*and." For a moment he hesitated about leaving his flag in the sack. Then he decided no, he would take it with him.

The Stirling bearing his stick was the first plane-load of invaders to take off from England shortly before midnight, June 5. Shortly thereafter, Marienne dropped through the hole in the plane's underside, becoming the first of the 185,000 Allied soldiers who would assault Hitler's Europe on D-Day.

The men of his stick were caught in the fire of a group of German soldiers on the ground, but Marienne got the survivors of the drop away and to their assigned rallying point.

There they discovered the Breton Resistance was anything but dead. Hundreds of FFI (French Forces of the Interior) fighters flocked to them, some armed, some not, some trained, some not. Before long, there were so many volunteers at Dickson that London flew in a massive arms drop and the SAS switched tactics.

Instead of sticking together in a unit, SAS men split up and became leaders of teams of the FFI. They began to cut bridges, blow up railway tunnels, ambush German vehicles, and create a general sense of insecurity all over Brittany. Finally, the Germans located their base and launched a massive attack against it with artillery and tanks. Its defenders held out until nightfall, then scattered into the countryside.

The SAS continued to lead small groups of FFI all across the peninsula, but instead of operating out of major bases, they began to function as independent groups. Marienne was prime among them, a kind of fleeting ghost, striking here, there, never sleeping in the same hideout two nights in a row.

The Gestapo in Brest had a devastatingly effective agent in its rank, a former French naval captain named Zeller.

"Get Marienne and any other SAS officer he could lay his hands on and kill them," was the order Zeller received from his Gestapo superiors.

His agents finally captured a wounded English SAS lieutenant named Gray. Gray was taken to Gestapo headquarters in Brest, stripped of his uniform and shot. One of Zeller's accomplices, another Frenchman who had Gray's rough age and build, took over the Englishman's uniform. At the head of a group of Germans and *milice* (often known as the French Gestapo) disguised as FFI fighters, they set off after Marienne.

One night in mid-July, they stumbled on an SAS/FFI camp not far from Brest. The Frenchman impersonating Gray told the FFI sentry he had to see Marienne.

"He's sleeping in that barn," the FFI guard said, pointing to a building down the road.

His throat was cut as a reward for his information.

The Frenchman acting for the Gestapo in his SAS

uniform then marched into the barn with his troop and routed Marienne and two others from their sleep.

"Pierre Marienne?" the Frenchman impersonating Gray asked.

Marienne sleepily acknowledged who he was.

That was his last gesture. He and his fellows were summarily executed where they lay, Marienne's head resting on his knapsack with its tricolor and the words "Vaincre et Mourir" written on it.

What a cruel irony—Pierre Marienne, the first Allied soldier, the first French soldier to land on the soil of France in the struggle for the nation's liberation—killed by a fellow Frenchman in the service of the Nazis Marienne had come to conquer.

USS Nevada firing her forward 14 guns off Normandy, June 6, 1944

14.

The Miracle of
D-Day—Surprise!

IT WAS, QUITE frankly, a miracle. There is no other word for it. It was only seconds after two thirty in the morning on Tuesday June 6, 1944, when, precisely on schedule, the ships of the invasion fleet began to come on station in the Bay of the Seine. There were over 5000 of them. Never before had the seas of this planet seen a comparable sight—and it was a spectacle that will almost surely never be repeated.

There were seven battleships, 23 cruisers, 250 other warships whose cannon would serve as floating artillery batteries to support the coming assault. There were thousands of transports crammed to their gunnels with the 150,000 troops scheduled to assault the shores of Hitler's Festung Europa before sunset; hospital ships, command ships, supply ships, freighters bearing tanks, half-tracks, and field guns.

Some of those ships had been at sea since June 1. They had sailed through storm and fog and raging seas. Yet they arrived off the Normandy Coast in good order, threading their way through the buoys and the now surfaced midget submarines pointing the way to their mooring points six to 11 miles off the seacoast, exactly as the naval commanders had planned.

The storm, which had almost stayed Eisenhower's hand, had granted the Allies the one element they had never expected the fortunes of war would offer them this day—surprise. Not a single German submarine, not an E Boat or an overflying reconnaissance plane or prying radar had detected that enormous fleet's presence. Only one of the 5000 ships had been lost in the passage.

At 0300, the men who would make up the first wave, elements of the 1st, 4th, and 29th U.S. Infantry Divisions, the 3rd Canadians, the 50th and 3rd British Infantry Divisions, with attached Rangers and Commandos, began to go over the sides of their transports into the landing craft that would run them onto the beach.

Many of those men had been at sea since June 1, living on C-Rations. Some were weak with fatigue and seasickness. Scrambling down the rope netting with their heavy packs was a hellish exercise. A Force Three wind was kicking the waters into an angry chop. Many of the waiting landing craft bobbed up and down on their davits like corks. Miscalculate the drop into the craft and a man could drown or be crushed between the landing craft and the mother ship. With the exception of a rare shaft of moonlight, it was pitch dark. Yet, except for the occasional clang of metal on metal or an angry curse from a GI who'd missed his footing, the only sounds came from the slap-slap of the seas and the moaning of the wind.

On shore, the German defenders along the coastline still were not aware that the armada was moored in the darkness before their gunports, that the invasion was about to break onto their beaches. Not a single artillery shell from the German batteries along the coast disturbed the preparations for the first wave's assault.

It would be another 90 minutes before the Germans would even discover that invasion fleet was upon them—and that discovery would come from that most primitive of listening devices, the human ear. A German sentry behind Utah Beach would finally sound the alarm after hearing the splash and clank of an anchor chain groping for a hold in five fathoms of water.

The first indications the German command had that something was happening in Normandy came a few minutes after 0100. at the headquarters of the 84th Corps in Saint-Lo. There the staff of the corps had quite literally just finished singing "Happy Birthday" to their commander, General Erich Marcks, and toasting their leader with champagne when a messenger burst in with the news that there was major Allied air activity over the Cherbourg Peninsula. By the time Marcks got down to his Operations Room, his phone was ringing. One of his commands informed him that British paratroopers were jumping on the eastern bank of the Orne River. It was not going to be a happy birthday for General Marcks.

At Rommel's headquarters at La Roche-Guyon, the Field Marshal's chief of staff, General Hans Helmut Speidel, was woken at 0230 with news of the paratrooper drop. Speidel dismissed its importance. It was probably, he told his staff, just an Allied effort to reinforce the Resistance. He did not bother to call Rommel sleeping at his home in Herrlingen.

Field Marshal Gerd Von Rundstedt, Rommel's superior as the Commander-in-Chief of the West, had retired at 2300 after finishing a good bottle of Bordeaux, as was his habit. His operations officer, General Bodo Zimmermann, the man who earlier in the evening had dismissed the famous warning of Verlaine's couplet, *"Les sanglots longs des violons de l'automne,"* decided to wake up the Field Marshal just before three. It was not something he did lightly. The marshal was rarely out of bed before the very un-military hour of 1000.

Von Rundstedt padded into his war room in his bedroom slippers and a bathrobe, clutching a cup of black coffee. He pondered the situation maps in silence for several minutes. Indolent von Rundstedt might have been, but there was nothing wrong with his military judgment once his mind started working. The parachute drops could very well be the opening phase of a major assault, he declared.

With that, he returned to his quarters to bathe, shave, and dress in his full uniform. He was too much the Prussian to take command of the western defenses of the Reich in a bathrobe.

Just before 0430, before the first Allied assault wave had even come ashore, the canny old Field Marshal made up his mind. The parachute drops were, indeed, the opening phase of what was going to be a major sea landing. They would have been designed to protect the landings' flanks, so the assault would have to come along the Norman shore between the Isigny and the Orne Rivers. Whether it would turn out to be a diversion or the invasion itself didn't matter. What mattered was preparing the ground for a major counter-attack.

He ordered the 12th SS Hitler Youth Panzer Division northeast of Caen and the Panzer Lehr Division near Orleans to start an immediate movement towards Normandy. It was exactly the right order to issue.

However, von Rundstedt did not have the authority to issue it. Only Hitler could order those reserves into action. Von Rundstedt decided to give the order anyway, then message Hitler's Headquarters informing them of what he done. If the two divisions got on the road quickly, the morning mists and the heavy cloud cover overhead would shield their movements from Allied air attack. They would be able to strike at the Allied landing beaches by mid-day. The deployment seemed such an obvious move to von Rundstedt that he was convinced even the generals at Hitler's headquarters, who he despised as simpletons, would have to agree.

They did not. When Hitler's Chief of Staff, General Alfred Jodl, woke up at 0630 and was informed of what the Field Marshal had done, he exploded. He immediately gave instructions that von Rundstedt's order was to be countermanded. The armoured divisions were not to move until Hitler gave the order. And the Fuhrer was sound asleep. Jodl did not consider the matter serious enough to justify waking him.

As a Field Marshal, von Rundstedt had the right to demand a telephone conversation with Hitler at any hour of the day or night. He could have picked up his phone and demanded to speak personally with the Fuhrer to get the two divisions released to his command. He did not. He held the "Bohemian corporal" in such utter contempt he rarely deigned to call him. Instead, he had breakfast and went out to his garden to putter with his roses.

Had those two divisions arrived to attack the chaos of the Allied beachhead on D-Day afternoon, no one can predict what devastation they might have wreaked on the Allied landings.

The assault began at 0530 with a roar of high explosives such as the Continent has never experienced before or since. Ten thousand aircraft, P51 Mustangs, Spitfires, Hurricanes, Lightnings swept in over the beaches at low altitude, rocketing, machine-gunning, and bombing the German defenders. High overhead, the Flying Fortresses, B26s, and Halifaxes of the 8th Air Force and Bomber Command showered high explosives onto the beaches. Offshore, the cannon of almost 600 warships began to lay down their covering fire.

To the men in the landing craft in the first wave, ready to move to their start lines, it was a reassuring sight. They could not know, of course, that over Omaha the visibility had been so bad the planes had decided to drop their bombs three miles inland. Not a single bomb fell on the beach's waiting defenders.

Shortly after 0530, while the pre-assault bombardment continued to shake the sky, the command came rasping out of the loud hailers in the transports: "Away all boats." The invasion of Europe was under way.

From boat to boat men shouted encouragement to each other, cheered to keep their spirits up: "US Rangers lead the way!" "Remember Dunkirk!" "For King and Country!"

One hundred and fifty thousand men would come ashore before sundown this day, but that first line of craft bouncing shoreward through the heavy seas carried just 3,000 men.

The first assault fell on Utah Beach because the tides ran earlier there. Behind the beach on which the landing was scheduled to strike, a row of 10-inch guns from the Maginot Line was dug into a high cliff. Below them and down to the level of the bluffs just beyond the high water mark were batteries of the feared German 88s, all sited to provide carefully interlocking fields of fire.

It was here that the second miracle of D-Day occurred. A heavy current churned by the storm and an error in the pilot boat took the incoming landing craft away from the fire of those defenders to a another strip of beach a mile to the south. It was lightly defended. There were no high bluffs and cliffs inland of the beaches that had to be scaled. The first attackers were on shore and into the dunes almost before the Germans could open fire.

The next two waves followed almost unopposed. To some of the men in those waves the landings seemed even easier than the tough training exercises they'd had back in England. Twenty-eight of the first waves' amphibious tanks got safely ashore.

The landing on that unscheduled and lightly defended beach posed only one problem. Immediately behind it were the waters of the 12-mile square artificial lake caused by Rommel's flooding. Only one causeway stretched inland over that lake from the beach. Should the invaders go for that causeway and bring the entire assault ashore through that narrow landward funnel? Or should the follow-up waves be sent in on the original beaches further north, which had three causeways from which they could exit inland?

Brigadier General Teddy Roosevelt, grandson of the pre-World War One president of the United States, the Deputy Commander of the 4th Division, made the decision—go for the single causeway and run the whole landing off the beach on which they'd been landed by mistake.

It was the right decision. By nightfall, the 4th would be six miles inland. The entire landing cost the division only 197 casualties. It was, said the American Ground Commander, General Omar Bradley, "A piece of cake."

That would not be true of the other beaches along the invasion front.

Troops land from USS LCI(L)-412 during the D-Day assault on Omaha Beach, June 6, 1944. Note half-track weapons carriers at the water's edge, with their guns pointing inland; troops dug in on the shore; and LCI(L)-412's bow 20mm gunner engaging enemy targets.

15.

Omaha,
Bloody Omaha

GRADUALLY, DAYLIGHT BEGAN to strip away the shades of night on Tuesday June 6, 1944. Mists rolling up from the sea helped obscure a shoreline already enveloped in the black, oily smoke rising from a thousand fires burning on shore. A pall of acrid gun smoke hung over the beaches, legacy of the 10,000 tons of high explosives that had thundered out of the sky as part of the unprecedented air and naval bombardment. Alas, as the attackers were soon to discover, that bombardment had done little more than stun the beach's German defenders in their well dug-in positions.

Promptly at 0630, the landing craft of the first assault wave started their run into the shore: the 2nd East Yorks onto Sword, the 3rd Canadians onto Juno, the Desert Rats of the British 50th Division onto Gold. With them came the green-bereted men of Lord Lovat's 4th Commando and Commandant Phillippe Kieffer's

Bataillon des Fusiliers Marines—known to their comrades as the French Commandos.

Despite the terrible grimness of the business ahead, the troops off the British beaches moved out with that splendidly British mixture of purposefulness and laughter, pomp and circumstance. Somewhere off Sword, a loudspeaker blared out "Roll Out the Barrel." Major C.K. King stood up in the bow of his 30-man landing craft and recited the King's speech from Shakespeare's *Henry V* for his troops:

> He that outlives this day and comes safe home
> Will stand a-tiptoe when this day is named.

As he concluded, his men—some of whom would not live out the next 15 minutes of this day—roared their approval.

Sword was expected to be the most heavily defended of the British beaches. The units going in had been warned to expect 50 percent casualties. The weight of the first wave went on Queen Beach, running from Lion-sur-Mer along Ouistreham Beach to Riva Bella jutting out to sea at the mouth of the Orne. The beach and the tidal flat were relatively short and flat. Inland, on a flat plain behind the beach, were lines of neat one- and two-story houses, the residences of the local population, or the summer homes of middle-class Parisians.

Many of them had been converted by the Germans into gun emplacements.

The 2nd East Yorkshire Regiment leading the assault took 200 casualties moving across the open beaches, but then found cover from German fire among the buildings immediately inland from the beaches. Moving from the cover of one building to the next, the men of the first wave started to knock out the Germans beach defenses, assaulting many of their strong points from behind. By 0830, with the exception of the occasional sniper, the beach had been largely cleared.

Here, the Frenchmen and women of the communities along the beach swarmed out of their homes to welcome the liberators ashore. On the beachfront itself a young French girl helped the wounded struggle away from the advancing tide. Bottles of wine and cider long saved for this day were passed to the happily astonished Englishmen. To cries of *"Vive les Anglais,"* the townspeople hugged and kissed the advancing troops. The mayor of Colleville-sur-Orne, resplendent in the tricolor sash and brightly polished helmet of *le Corps du Sapeurs-Pompiers* (firemen) came down to the beach to formally welcome the troops ashore.

The toughest landing on the British beaches was for the Canadians at Juno Beach, a few miles west of Sword. Rough seas delayed the first wave's run on to the beach and a late tide exposed a reef at the western end that forced the first landing craft into a narrow strip in the heart of the German defenses. Twenty of the 24 vessels in that first wave were lost. Artillery support for the landing was supposed to be provided by ancient British Centaur tanks mounting 95mm Howitzers. Like the other tanks coming onto the British beaches, they'd been wrapped in a sort of inflatable rubber girdle that was supposed to prevent them from sinking as they moved from their landing craft to the dry shore.

They didn't work on the top-heavy old tanks. Thirty-four of them were lost to the rough seas. Still the Canadians fought their way inland. At Courseulles and Saint-Aubin they faced something the other D-Day attackers didn't have to face: house to house and street to street fighting in a built-up area. Still, by afternoon they'd cleared the towns and were moving off toward their objective, the Caen-Bayeux highway.

Like the landings at Sword, the landings of the 1st Hampshires and the 1st Dorsets on Gold encountered less opposition than the planners had anticipated. Here the inventiveness of the British engineers paid off. Particularly valuable were their flail tanks, which whacked at the sands with chain metal flails, exploding hidden land mines. The second great success was the "Roly-Poly," a long strip of rolled-up metal that could be unrolled along the beach to provide traction for wheeled vehicles as they passed over the sand on their way to hard ground.

It was at the next beach, however, that disaster almost befell the Allied assault.

Omaha, bloody Omaha—the name of that 6000-yard strip of sand was about to enter U.S. lore beside the names of the Civil War battlefields of Antietam, Chancellorsville, and Bloody Angle. It was a name that would become synonymous with fighting as intense, as murderous, as any endured by the U.S. Marines in their assaults on Tarawa, Pelieu, and Iwo Jima in the Pacific.

With its line of bluffs rising up from the beaches to heights of 200 feet, Omaha had the best natural defensive positions in the invasion area. It also had the best defenders. Unbeknownst to the Allied planners, the beach's second-rate 716th Infantry Division had been reinforced by two regiments of the veteran 352nd Division. Finally, at Omaha, the invasion fleet had to anchor 12 miles at sea, compared to six miles on the other invasion beaches. That was because it was feared the six, 155mm guns on the Pointe du Hoc could, with their 25,000-yard range, savage the fleet if it moved in any closer.

What that meant, of course, was that the naval gunfire supporting the troops at Omaha would be far less accurate and far less powerful than the gunfire at any of the other beaches.

The initial assault on Omaha was to be led by 1,450 men in 36 landing craft, the men of the 16th

Regimental Combat Team of the 1st Division and the 116th Regimental Combat Team of the 29th Infantry Division. The landing strip had been divided into three beaches, Easy, Dog, and Fox, each with three sub-beaches, Red, Green, and White.

At 0525, 32 amphibious tanks were supposed to come on shore and take up positions at the water's edge to cover the assault waves' landings.

Five minutes later, another 24 tanks were to come ashore from Landing Craft Tanks (LCTs).

One minute later, the assault troops were to land.

Two minutes later, 270 men of the underwater demolition teams were to clear 50-yard paths through the mines of Rommel's Devil's Garden for the main assault waves, which would head in at 0700.

That was the plan. It didn't work. Nothing on Omaha Beach that June day was going to work according to plan.

The aerial bombardment had, because of poor visibility, landed three miles inland. Not a single bomb had fallen on the beach's German defenders. The naval bombardment deafened men in their bunkers and set the undergrowth along the high bluffs ablaze. All that did was make accurate follow-up naval gunfire impossible. Otherwise, the bombardment did virtually nothing to the beach's defenses. The German gun emplacements had been built to be immune to direct fire from the sea. They were.

Unaware that the bombardment had left the beach's defenders unscathed, the 36 landing craft of the first wave set out.

They were heading for a disaster.

As they approached, the Germans held back, waiting until they were well within range before exposing their positions by firing. Then they opened up, first their machine guns with traversing fire, their arcs of fire all designed to interlock, then the heavy guns from their bunkers along the bluffs above the beach.

In their landing craft, the frightened and seasick men could hear the machine gun fire beating its metallic tattoo on the flanks of their landing craft. As the crafts lowered their ramps and they struggled out into the surf with their 100-pound packs, the machine guns' fire churned the water around them.

Some men in their haste to get out of the landing craft leapt over the side and drowned. With their enormous packs, in water up to their chests, those who got off the landing craft ramps alive had to struggle over the uneven footing of the runnels crisscrossing the tidal flat. They moved with the agonizing slowness of figures in a nightmare, toy dolls in a shooting gallery for the German machine gunners on the bluffs above them.

For those who made it, exhausted, to the water's edge, there were another 200 yards of open beach to cross under that murderous fire before they could find shelter at the base of the bluffs. One company of 64 Rangers lost 35 men in that sprint from the water's edge to the bluff.

Only five of the 32 tanks that were supposed to land to give the infantry support fire made it to the beach. Three out of 16 bulldozers made it; not a single piece of artillery did.

The 270 engineers who were supposed to clear lanes through the mines of Rommel's Devil's Garden for the second wave were cut down by the same intense machine gun fire that had savaged the infantry of the first wave. In just 30 minutes, they lost almost half their strength.

At 0700 the second wave came in to that same savage gunfire, onto a beachfront that had not been cleared of mines. The disaster was compounded. All up and down the beach there was chaos and confusion. Officers were separated from their men, squads from their platoons, platoons from their companies. Virtually no one was in front of the positions they had been trained to recognize and attack.

Naval support fire was impossible—the beach was shrouded with so much smoke the gunners couldn't pick out targets. Leaderless men huddled at the base of the bluff, paralyzed by fear and indecision. On Dog Green Beach the machine guns' fire was so murderous some men ran back to the water's edge and lay in the waves as though somehow the sea's green shroud might protect them from death. Others dropped into the surf and waited to crawl forward with the advancing tide. By mid-morning, the Omaha beachhead was little more than a few hundred yards of corpse-littered sand. Along parts of Dog Red and Dog Green Beaches, the nightmare that had haunted the sleep of Winston Churchill had come true: the surf splashing onto Omaha's sands was tinged pink with the blood of the dozens of young Americans who had already died in its foaming waters.

On his command ship the Augusta, the American ground commander General Omar Bradley despaired that the Allies had suffered "an irreversible catastrophe," the sort of disaster to justify the worst fears of Churchill and Sir Alan Brooke. He began to contemplate directing the remaining waves that were supposed to go onto Omaha to Utah, and evacuating Omaha. This action which would have left an enormous 20-mile wide gap in the Allied lines that would have been a disaster in the making for the landings.

As he despaired, however, the situation on the beach began to turn. The more experienced men of the 1st Infantry Division, the Big Red One, reacted first. Those troops, Bradley would later say, saved the day. Gradually, small groups of men began to pick their way up the bluffs, knocking out the German positions in their way as they advanced.

The senior officers marched up and down the beaches, inspiring by their personal courage and inspiration the stunned and frightened men.

"Two kinds of people are going to stay on this beach," Colonel George A. Taylor of the 116th Infantry Regiment shouted at his troopers, "the dead and those who are about to die. Now let's get the hell out of here!"

And his men began to do just that.

Brigadier General Norman Cota of the 29th Division stomped up and down the beach chewing on a dead Dutch Masters cigar, exhorting his men to move forward.

"Who are you?" he yelled at one group of men.

"Rangers," was the answer.

"Then, God damn it, if you're Rangers get up and lead the way."

Prodded by men like Cota and Taylor and other unheralded noncoms and junior officers, the men began to move. There were five exits off the beach. Shortly after noon, two of them had been forced open, one by blasting through its defenses with Bangalore torpedoes, the other by assaulting the positions covering it from the rear.

At last, at 1330, General Leonard T. Gerow, commanding the V Corps, could radio to Bradley, "the troops formerly pinned down on the beaches…advancing up the heights behind the beach."

It had been a near run thing, the closest the Allies had come to disaster on D-Day. Over 2,000 GI's died on that strip of sand. For the rest of his life, the memory of what happened on Omaha Beach on June 6, 1944 would pain Omar Bradley. "Every man who set foot on Omaha Beach that day," he was to write, "was a hero."

An American Soldier lies dead alongside an anti-landing craft obstruction on Omaha Beach, June 6, 1944.

16.

The Pointe du Hoc–Futile Heroism

STATISTICS. SO MUCH of the vast enterprise that was the Normandy landings is summed up today in superlatives and statistics—the largest this, the biggest that. The first one of its kind.

All very true, of course, but behind each of those statistics lies a human face. There are the distinct identities of the men and women who gave those statistics meaning, there are the acts of individual courage and devotion that were the bricks and mortar of the landings' success. Above all, there is the sacrifice of those unknown young men whose lives ended there in the brief fury of that June morning so long ago.

Key among those who assaulted the Point de Hoc were the 177 men of the *Commandos Fusiliers-Marins*, the first soldiers of France since 1940 to fight the occupant on the soil of the *patrie* in French uniforms, and the men of the 2nd and 5th Rangers.

The French were a small, elite company—less than 300 men served in the battalions ranks. Founded at Camberley in April, 1941, every man in the battalion was a volunteer. From their founding, they had been led by one man, Commandant Phillippe Kieffer, a veteran of the evacuation of Dunkirk who had never shed his French officer's uniform.

His commandos had fought at Dieppe and led numerous raids on the coast of Occupied France. Their physical training in England was as rigorous, as demanding as that undergone by any unit in the Second World War. Few men were better trained for what awaited them on D-Day than Kieffer's commandos, known to their English allies as "the Free French Marines."

In April, they were attached to the 1st Commando Brigade of Brigadier Lord Lovat, a colorful, much decorated Scottish peer of the realm. The Brigade was composed of four Commandos, the 3rd, 4th, 6th Commandos and the 45th Royal Marines. The French were assigned to the 4th Commandos, made up of seven troops—three French and four British—some 600 men in all.

Lovat, who knew and loved France, decided the three French troops should have the honor of being the first members of his commando brigade onto French soil. On the evening of the June 4, after the troops had all been briefed on their missions for D-Day, Lovat assembled his brigade.

"We attack in our green berets," he announced. Commandos were too proud to go ashore in the steel pot of the infantry soldier. The Frenchmen boarded their landing barges, Nos. 526 and 527, at Warsash on the Hamble River at 1730, Monday, June 5th, with martial airs from a hand-wound phonograph piping them onto their barges.

They would not be coming back. Their orders, Kieffer stated were, "*s'accrocher, rester ou mourir*" ("dig in, hold on or die").

By sunset, they were off the Isle of Wight in pitching seas, swept up in the vast circling armada of the invasion fleet. Just before midnight Kieffer went below decks to see his men for a last time. Many were already reeling with seasickness from the tossing of their flat-bottomed barge.

Worried by what that might mean in a few hours' time, Kieffer wrapped himself up in a blanket to get some sleep. As he did, he murmured to himself the words of Sir John Astley's prayer on the eve of the battle Newbury:

"Lord I shall be very busy this day. I may forget thee, but do not thou forget me."

At four-thirty, the men were up; at five they were on deck straining for their first glimpse of the shorelines of home. They were supposed to land in front of a *colonie de vacances* at a place called La Breche on Ouistreham Plage. From there, if they got ashore in the right place, they were to move along the waterfront highway toward Colleville-sur-Orne, assault the town of Ouistreham, capture its port and, above all, the (intact) locks at the mouth of the Orne Canal.

To do it, they would have to attack and destroy from behind the heavily fortified German positions along the waterfront and particularly the old gambling casino at Riva Bella, converted by the Germans into the anchor of their defense line.

Staring off into the darkness, trying to make out the oncoming shore, Count Guy Vourch, a captain commanding one of Kieffer's three troops, thought how appropriate that it was he who would be assaulting that casino. He had left, after all, a considerable sum of his modest family fortune on its tables before the war.

Suddenly at 0645, the shoreline erupted in blinking red and yellow lights. To some of the landing barges it seemed as though the display panel of a gigantic pinball machine had just erupted before them. Minutes later, just after the two barges threw down their landing ramps, a 75mm shell tore the ramp off No. 526. The men on board had no choice but leap over the sides into two meters of water with their heavy packs and scramble for the shore.

The run from the water's edge across the beach to the shelter of the line of houses just across the seaside road was the most dangerous part of the operation. Fifty-seven of the commandos 177 men, including four of its 13 officers, fell crossing that 200-yard wide strip of beach. Yet, the commandos' orders were strict—leave the wounded where they'd fallen and press ashore. Caring for the wounded was the responsibility of the men of the second wave.

Hubert Faure, a young NCO stepping into action for the first time, would recall *"que ce fut dur de voir les camarades, les bons copains tomber autour de soi—entendre leurs cris de souffrance et d'etre oblige de les abandonner dans l'eau rouge de leur sang."* ("How hard it was to see comrades, good pals falling around you—to hear their suffering cries and yet be obliged to leave them in water reddened by their blood.")

As the young Frenchman continued up the beach, he was moved to tears by the sight of one of the wounded waving them on, singing "La Marseillaise."

One of the commando's most popular officers, Pierre "Pepe" Dumenoir, managed to struggle from the water's edge to the roadside so that he could lie down to die with his eyes looking south to Paris.

By 0815, the 114 survivors of the dash over the beach assembled on their rallying point, the *colonie des vacances*, and began to move onto Ouistreham, leapfrogging from building to building along the inland side of the seaside road and tramline, which put them behind the Germans' waterfront fortifications.

While the men of one troop, led by Lieutenant Amaury, provided covering fire, the men of the other two troops moved up on the Germans' strongpoint, the old gambling casino at Riva Bella. A pair of 20mm cannons on the concrete reinforced roof of the casino poured fire into the advancing Frenchmen.

Two efforts to knock the guns out with PIAT (Projector. Infantry, Anti-Tank) weapons produced only wounded French commandos.

Finally, hearing that half a dozen Centaur tanks had gotten ashore to support the commandos, Kieffer himself set out to round one up. He was back with his tank at 0925, clutching to its turret to direct its fire. A hundred and fifty yards from the casino, he was hit in the arm, his second wound of the day. The tank blasted out the twin 20mm guns with a dozen rounds.

Kieffer's commandos moved in to assault the casino immediately. The tank followed, blowing apart one of the casino's towers from which heavy fire was holding up the French advance.

By 1120 it was over. The casino was out of action, the locks at the entry to the canal had been seized intact. And at what a price! Over a third of those green-bereted Frenchmen who'd plunged ashore from their barges four hours earlier had been killed or wounded. Still, a pair of teenagers from the town looked on in wonder.

"Boy, are those British smart!" one said admiringly.

"They send guys over here who speak French just as well as we do."

The day's fighting was not yet over for the French commandos, however. They formed up with the rest of the brigade to work their way up the banks of the Orne River to relieve the men of the 6th Airborne who'd seized the bridges over the river and the Caen Canal shortly after midnight.

Major John Howard and his men, under constant German attack for hours, were due to be relieved, according the D-Day plan, at 1230.

Suddenly, to the utter amazement of Howard, his men, and the Germans attacking them, Lovat and his commandos appeared on the horizon.

"Laddie," Lovat told his bagpiper Bill Millin, "Give us, 'Blue Bonnets Over the Border.'"

With the piper's notes skirling away, Lovat and his commandos came marching over the bridge to the paras on the other side. For a minute or two even the Germans were too stunned to fire.

Halfway across, the piper looked back at their commander. He was striding along confidently, as if inspecting the fields of his estate. At the far end of the bridge, Major Howard rushed out to greet his relief. Lovat glanced at his watch.

"Dreadfully sorry, old chap," he said to Howard. "We're two-and-a-half minutes late."

On the western end of the landing beaches, the 2nd and 5th Rangers of Lieutenant Colonel Jim Rudder were assigned what to any sane man would have appeared an impossible task—they had exactly 30 minutes to scale cliffs 100 feet high—as tall as a nine-story building—at the Pointe du Hoc and knock out the German gun batteries atop the cliff. The same long-range guns that had forced the Omaha Beach invasion fleet to anchor 12 miles offshore.

Using grappling irons and rope, working their way up those heights foot by bloody foot, in the face of German defenders who could lob hand grenades on them

U.S. Army Rangers rest atop the cliffs at Pointe du Hoc, which they stormed in support of Omaha Beach landings on D-Day, June 6, 1944.

like rocks, the Rangers got to the top. They lost half their company doing it, but they got there.

But the guns they had come to destroy were not there.

They were a mile-and-a-half inland, not yet installed in their cement bunkers. Jean Marion, a young French Resistant, had spotted them and tried, unsuccessfully, to get the information to London.

The Rangers' assault was, with the British attack on the Merville gun battery, the outstanding feat of arms in the D-Day fighting. It was also, alas, the most futile achievement of that terrible morning.

17.

D-Day—The
Germans React

IT WAS ALL happening at this very moment, more than 60 years ago, Tuesday June 6, 1944. At 0730, the men of the Allied armies were struggling onto the beaches they were soon to sanctify with their blood and heroism—Sword, Juno, Gold, Omaha, Utah.

On some of those beaches, the fighting would be surprisingly easy, success swifter than General Eisenhower's planners could have hoped. On others, like Omaha, the fighting was as savage, the losses as severe, as they were anywhere in the Second World War.

How about the Germans? How did their high command react to the landings? The Allies had, thanks to the storm that had swept the Channel June 5, received one unexpected gift from the Gods of War—surprise. They were about to get another from their enemies' high command.

For Colonel Baron Alexis von Roenne, Tuesday, June 6, 1944 would represent the culmination of a lifetime of service to the German Army. At mid-morning, he received a personal call from Hitler's Chief of Staff, General Alfred Jodl. Jodl had just left a conference in the Fuhrer's bedroom. The Fuhrer, Jodl said, wanted von Roenne's best appraisal of the Allied landings ready for his mid-day strategy conference. Hitler himself had assigned von Roenne to his job as head of *Fremde Heere West*—Foreign Army's West, the branch of the Wehrmacht Intelligence responsible for analyzing the strengths and intentions of the Allies—because he held the Prussian aristocrat's judgement in such high esteem.

Fortunately, von Roenne had on his desk that morning a freshly delivered package from the headquarters of the Abwehr, the German Intelligence Service on Berlin's Tirpitzstrasse. It contained the intelligence reports the Abwehr had received in the past week from one of its two best secret agents in England, V-Mann Armand. That material was a godsend for von Roenne. It provided a framework into which he could now fit much of the raw data that had flowed across his desk in the past fortnight.

It was not the Divine, however, who had sent that material to von Roenne. It was the Allies' deception experts implementing their Plan Fortitude. V-Mann Armand was, in fact, the Polish Air Force Officer operating under the strict control of Britain's MI5 counter-intelligence service.

Von Roenne began his Situation Report West No. 1288—it survived the war—with a very accurate appraisal of the fighting front in Normandy only four hours after the first troops had come ashore. The landings, he remarked, "can hardly have lived up to the expectations of the enemy. His bridgehead is shallow in its depth in some places and lacks an efficient port."

Then, describing his source as "a believable Abwehr report of June 2," he detailed the breakdown of the Allied forces in England, the 21st Army Group of Field Marshal Montgomery making the Normandy landings, and the non-existent 1st U.S. Army Group of General George Patton, opposite Calais.

"Not a single unit of the First U.S. Army Group, which comprises approximately 25 large formations, has so far been committed," he noted. That clearly demonstrated, von Roenne pointed out, that "the enemy is planning a further large-scale operation in the Channel area, which one would expect to be aimed at a coastal sector in Pas-de-Calais."

A million ghosts, the members of that non-existent army of Plan Fortitude, had just gone into history in what was without any doubt the single most important German intelligence appreciation of the Second World War.

Hitler's mid-day strategy conference that day was held at the Castle Klessheim, an hour's drive from Berchtesgaden in the Hohensalzburg Mountains where he was hosting a luncheon for his new Hungarian satrap, General Dome Sztojay. With what satisfaction he should have contemplated his war maps that day! After all, the Allies had come ashore in Normandy, exactly where he had told his dubious generals and Field Marshals they would at his March 19 strategy conference.

He was laughing, almost carefree, thought Albert Speer, his industrial czar who attended the meeting.

"Now," Hitler boasted, "we have them where we can destroy them."

Yet something very strange happened at that conference, something that has never been explained.

The Abwehr had received a blizzard of reports on the Allies' landing intentions. One of them came from an agent in Casablanca. He said the Allies would land in Normandy on June 6. Hitler had seen that report. Was it the report that had caused him to order Normandy reinforced in mid-May? No one knows.

And who did it come from? Was it a Vichy agent who had somehow gotten hold of a secret few Frenchmen possessed? Was it simply a freelance agent blowing smoke at his Abwehr controller for a few Deutschmarks? Once again, no one knows the answer to that either.

What is known is the astonishing effect that uncannily accurate report had on Hitler's suspicious mind that morning of June 6, 1944. Speer recorded it in his diary.

It was a lure, Hitler told Speer, an Allied trick to divert his attention from the real threat facing him. Furthermore, it confirmed von Roenne's analysis. The man who, against the collective wisdom of his generals had fingered Normandy as the landing site, now changed his mind.

"My opinion," he announced, "is that this is not the real invasion yet."

Then, cheerfully proclaiming, "We're off," he stepped into his mid-day strategy conference. He was, his Deputy Chief of Operations General Walter Warlimont noted in his diary, chuckling in a carefree manner as he studied the situation maps his staff had prepared for him.

A little too carefree, perhaps. There was one critical decision that had to be taken at that conference, a decision that should have been taken hours before, the decision to release to von Rundsted's command the two Panzer divisions the Field Marshal had wanted marching on Normandy before dawn. Hitler refused to make that decision. He would mull it over during his vegetarian lunch.

Finally, after two o'clock, Hitler emerged from his lunch and authorized the release of the Hitler Youth and Panzer Lehr to von Rundstedt's command. But that was all the old Field Marshal was going to get. Not a tank, not a soldier of the reserves in the area behind the 15th Army in the Pas-de-Calais was to be moved. That decision taken, Hitler went back to the Berghof to take a nap.

By the time his orders reached the two Panzers, it was well after four o'clock in the afternoon. When von Rundstedt had given them the orders to move, there was an hour of pre-dawn darkness left. Until close to mid-day, the storm clouds still passing over the Cotentin would have helped to protect their advance from Allied fighter attacks.

Now, the Allied fighters were prowling the air again. There was no question of beginning any movement towards the beaches until darkness had fallen.

There was only one serious German counter-attack on that day on which Rommel had vowed to defeat the Allied Invasion at the water's edge. And even that came puzzlingly late in the day. The closest armoured unit to the invasion beaches was the veteran 21st Panzer, once a part of Rommel's Afrika Corps. Its tanks and men were quartered in farms and villages scattered over a 25-mile square area south and east of Caen where Allied fighter planes couldn't find them.

The division had gone on alert after two in the morning when the reports of the first Allied airdrops came in. For hours the men had been sitting beside or in their vehicles, their engines often running, waiting for the orders to move out. None came.

That was due in part, at least, to the confused chain of command under which the division fell. It involved Rommel's Army Group "B," von Rundstedt's OB West, and a special armoured command, Panzer Group West, each of which had some responsibility for armoured moves in France. In the tension of the hours following the landing, there was apparently a tendency for each command to assume the other had ordered the division forward.

No one had. It wasn't until late in the afternoon that the 124 tanks of the divisions' 22nd Panzer regiment were ordered to assault the Allied landings. Fortunately, they moved against the Allied positions nearest to their assembly point, the men of the 3rd British Division who'd come ashore at Sword Beach, and by mid-afternoon were already well dug in. General Erich Marcks, the commander of the 84th Corps, the man whose birthday this day was, came to see the attack off.

"Oppeln," he told the regiment's commander, Colonel Hermann von Oppeln-Bronikowski, a pre-war Olympic rider, "the future of Germany may very well rest on your shoulders."

One section of Bronikowski's tanks plunged due north from the little Norman village of Lebisey, rolling right into the yawning gap between the English troops on

Sword Beach and the Canadians on Juno. Thirty-seven tanks under Captain Wilhelm von Gottberg assaulted towards Periers on a ridge-line running parallel to the shore four miles from the sea. Bronikowski took another 25 tanks to strike the crossroads village of Bieville.

Von Gottberg's tanks ran head-on into the well dug-in forward positions of the Staffordshire Regiment. The English anti-tank fire was deadly. Within 20 minutes, 13 of the 37 German tanks were ablaze. That was enough for von Gottberg. He withdrew to dig his surviving tanks into defensive positions around Caen. Bronikowski fared little better. Those British gunners had scored a stunning triumph. By nightfall only 54 of the regiment's 124 tanks were still functioning.

A handful, however, did reach the Channel shore at Lion-sur-Mer, where they found men of the German 716th Infantry Regiment still dug into their strongpoints. They had uncovered a terrible Allied secret—that yawning gap between the British and Canadian lines. Drive an armoured division into that hole and start attacking their Allied beachheads on the flanks and the result could have been a disaster.

Thanks to Adolf Hitler, however, there were no German Panzer divisions around to exploit that opening.

And if they had been? What difference would they have made? General Max Pemsel, who commanded the 7th Army in Normandy, had little doubt. They would have won the day. In an interrogation after the war, he said a joint attack by those two divisions, plus the 21st "would have been able to pretty well liquidate the British landing, and the following day three additional divisions from the 15th Army area could have been made available for a massive counter-attack on the American bridgehead and what was left of the British."

Battles are not won, however, nor is history written by "what if's" but by what was. The divisions weren't there and the handful of tanks that had reached the sea pulled back when a heavy glider flight passed over them, convincing their commander that they were about to be cut off from behind.

And what of Field Marshal Rommel, the man who was going to crush the Allies at the water's edge this day?

His command post did not even bother to call him at his home in Herrlinghen until 1030 in the morning. He immediately called his Aide-de-Camp, Captain Helmuth Lang, with the order to get his car ready for an immediate departure for France. "Imagine, Lang," he said in a tone of voice he might have used to announce the death of a good friend, "the great day has come. The Allies are landing in Normandy and we are here."

By noon, he was ready for the race back to his headquarters. A few minutes after his Horche sped out of his driveway, his wife Lucie went up to her bedroom to try on the gray shoes he had brought her from Paris for her birthday. There she came upon the last stroke of bad luck that would befall the Field Marshal this day.

The shoes didn't fit.

Like so many husbands, Rommel didn't know his wife's shoe size.

Thanks to clever misinformation, the Germans believed General George S. Patton was stationed in England with his (non-existent) 1st U.S. Army Group.

18.

D-Day Night—All Still There To Play For

FOR THE ALLIES as for the Germans, the longest day was almost over. As the sun began to set through the haze of the invasion front half a century ago, its final rays picked out the terrible shambles of battle: the destroyed landing craft littering the tidal flats, the burned-out and destroyed tanks, half-tracks and trucks scattered over the beaches, the rubble of German fortifications and the ruins of hundreds of homes of the Normans who had paid such a heavy price for their nation's coming liberation.

At water's edge on Bloody Omaha, a few of the bodies of the Americans who had died there continued to bob on the tide.

Still, the measure of the Allies' achievements on this day came down to one figure—155,000 Allied soldiers had gotten on shore since the first paratroopers had begun their drops shortly after midnight—83,115 British and Canadian soldiers, 72,000 Americans. They had paid a price—12,000 dead and wounded. Heavy though they were, those losses had been less than the Allied planners had anticipated, thanks to the storm, which had nearly prompted General Eisenhower to postpone the invasion. That tempest had given the attackers the one advantage no one had ever expected them to have—surprise.

Nowhere, however, had the Allied operations gone exactly to plan. Omaha had come close to being a disaster. By sunset, the landing area was barely a mile-and-a-half deep around Colleville—and that was the deepest penetration the Americans had been able to make. At Saint-Laurent, they didn't even hold a beachhead a mile deep. There were still German strongpoints behind the Americans' forward positions. The entire area was under German artillery fire.

Almost half of the tanks and half-tracks that had been scheduled to come ashore had been lost. Two thousand four hundred tons of supplies were supposed to have been landed during the day; barely a hundred had made it. The beach was so strewn with rubble and wrecked vehicles that new landings were agonizingly slow.

The 4th U.S. Infantry Division, by contrast, had driven six miles inland off Utah Beach. They had landed 22,000 men and 1,800 vehicles. Their troops had linked up with those of the 101st Airborne. However, the operations of the 101st and the 82nd on the base of the Cotentin had been limited by the fact they'd been dropped over such a scattered area. Many of their vital objectives had not been attained, and in particular, the bridges over the Merderet River.

The 82nd Airborne was holding onto Ste-Mère-Église and thus firmly astride the highway to Cherbourg, but the town was still under heavy German pressure. There was, the Corps Commander General J. Lawton "Lightning Joe" Collins admitted, "a great deal of confusion and lack of control in the area."

To the east, the situation on the British beaches was considerably better. The 6th Airborne had seized the passages over the Orne River and secured the invasions' flank.

The 9th Brigade of the 3rd Infantry Division, the last unit to land on Sword, had charged straight inland and captured its D-Day objective, the Carpiquet Airfield.

The 3rd Infantry, as a whole, however, had been given as its objective for the day seizing the city of Caen. It was probably a much too ambitious assignment. The division hadn't even come close to taking it. By nightfall, the tanks of the 21st Panzer Division, which had survived the 3rd Division's deadly gunnery during their earlier counter-attack, and the remains of the 716th German Infantry Division, had taken up strong defensive positions on the city's outskirts. That night, the first advance elements of the 12th SS Panzer Division moved into the city. It would be weeks before it would fall to the Allies.

The Canadians coming off Juno had cut the Caen Bayeux highway. All told, theirs was probably the most successful of the D-Day landings.

Everywhere, however, as the sun of D-Day set, the Allies were, Chester Wilmot, the British historian wrote, "tired and strung out in a series of hastily prepared positions...their line was thin and there were gaps which cried out for exploration."

There was, as the Germans already knew, a yawning gap between the Canadian and British positions around Luc and Lion-sur-Mer and an even bigger gap between the Americans still bottled up on Omaha Beach and Utah Beach. Get a German Panzer Division into either of those holes and the Allied landing was going to be in a very dangerous situation.

On May 25, in his final pre-invasion briefing for the King, Winston Churchill and all his generals, Field Marshal Sir Bernard Montgomery had warned that if on the evening of D-Day the Allies did not hold Caen, Bayeux, and Carentan, then their landing "would be very awkwardly placed, indeed."

As the sun set June 6, 1944, they did not hold one of those objectives—not one.

Well after dark, Field Marshal Gerd von Rundstedt summoned his principal aides to a conference in the operations room of his headquarters for the Western Front at Saint-Germain-en-Laye. The last Teutonic Knight had spent the day far from the din and the ignoble strife of the battlefield in the serene contemplation of his maps and intelligence reports.

Indeed, fuming at the refusal of Hitler's headquarters to release him the Hitler Youth and 12th SS Panzer Divisions before dawn, he had passed a good deal of the invasion morning puttering in his garden.

General Gunther von Blumentritt, his Chief of Staff, opened the meeting by informing him of the growing conviction of *Fremde Heere West*, the Wehrmacht's Western Front Intelligence Centre, and of Hitler's headquarters that Normandy was a diversion, a feint designed to force a premature German reaction.

The old Field Marshal digested that, studied his war map for a minute or two and decreed that Hitler, his generals, and the intelligence experts were wrong.

There was going to be no second landing. Normandy was the invasion, all of it that there was ever going to be. He pointed to his map. The immense swath of coastline the Allies had attacked indicated that they were preparing for an enormous build-up.

Look at the divisions they were using in the attack, he said—the First U.S., the British Desert Rats, the 6th Airborne, the 82nd. They were the best divisions the Allies had. Were they going to waste those divisions on a diversion? Never.

The time had now come, he proclaimed, for Hitler to free up all his available forces, and especially the Panzers of the 15th Army massed behind the Pas-de-Calais, and start them on the way to Normandy. It was, of course, the one thing the Allies did not want the Fuhrer to do.

The critical time for the Allies was beginning, von Rundstedt said. Their losses had been heavy. They were clinging to a weak and isolated bridgehead. Their supply line was still not assured. This was the moment to strike.

Classical military doctrine held, the Field Marshal knew, that the success or failure of an invasion bridgehead depended on whether or not the invader could reinforce his bridgehead by sea faster than the defender could bring up his reinforcements by land. It was a race, and it was a race that von Rundstedt and Germany could win, provided Hitler allowed him to move quickly.

There was a plan already drawn up for just this contingency. It was called Case IIIA.

Inform Hitler and his headquarters that the time had come to implement it, he ordered his staff. Start moving forces out of Calais and on to Normandy.

Having unburdened himself of his judgement with all the serene conviction of a Pope reading out a Papal encyclical, the Field Marshal went off to bed.

At about the same time, an hour's drive from his headquarters, the longest day in the life of Field Marshal Erwin Rommel was drawing to a close. Shortly after ten, his Horche skidded to a halt in front of the chateau of the Dukes of La Rochefoucauld at La Roche-Guyon. His

Aide, Captain Helmut Lang, leapt out and rushed inside to alert his Chief of Staff, General Hans Speidel, that Rommel was back. A Wagnerian overture's ponderous notes swelled through the chateau corridors.

"The Allies are landing and you are playing music?" Lang shouted.

Speidel fixed him with a dour glare. "Do you think that will change anything?" he asked.

Rommel went immediately to the officer's mess to confer with his staff. Did he notice that the domestics of the Duke of La Rochefoucauld had discreetly removed the priceless Gobelins Tapestry that usually graced the mess's walls during the day?

Colonel Anton Staubwasser, his Intelligence Officer, informed him that Colonel von Roenne of *Fremde Heere West* had called at 1720 to warn that a second major assault in the Pas-de-Calais was to be expected shortly.

His words were far more soothing to Rommel's ears than the strains of Wagner had been. He had promised he would defeat the Allies at water's edge, but when they'd waded ashore that morning, he'd been 500 miles away sound asleep.

Nothing would have pleased him more than a second Allied assault on the Calais beaches where he had been predicting they would attack for months. There he would stop them at the water's edge. It was not the moment to take a single soldier or tank out of the Pas-de-Calais.

An air of serene detachment apparently characterized Hitler's evening strategy conference that night. It was much too early to order Case IIIA, he said. He did not seem unduly upset by the Allies' initial successes in Normandy. Instead, he spent a quiet night listening to Strauss and Wagner before going to bed.

U.S. Army Rangers show off the ladders they used to storm the cliffs at Pointe du Hoc, which they assaulted in support of Omaha Beach landings on D-Day, June 6, 1944.

On the invasion beaches, the men of the Allied forces did what infantrymen always do. They dug their holes, propped their weapons on the edges of those holes, wrapped themselves in a blanket or poncho, chewed on their cold rations, and fell into the sleep of the utterly exhausted.

"There had been little doubt," one of the architects of Plan Fortitude wrote after the war, "that we would get ashore. Where the doubts arose were whether or not we would be able to stay ashore."

For the Allies as well as for the Germans, the critical days and hours—the days and hours that would determine whether the Normandy landings would succeed or end in a bloody disaster—were now beginning.

As the British historian of the landing wrote in the idiom of the cricket pitch, on that night of June 6-7, 1944: "It was all still there to play for."

19.

Liberation's Painful Price

CASUALTIES ARE, ALAS, the human fertilizer which have, since time immemorial, nourished the battlefield. Throughout much of history, the victims on the battlefield were limited to the combatants themselves who fought upon those fields. The civilians paid their price later, in the acts of rape, pillage, and slaughter often imposed on them by the victors.

With this century and the introduction of modern armaments, the civilian, the non-combatant, has been called on, willingly or unwillingly, to share the sacrifices of war with the soldier on the battlefront.

The celebrations of the Normandy Landings focus quite properly on the men who fought on the Norman beaches, on their struggles and their sacrifices.

But what about the sacrifices of the people of Normandy, of those men, women, and children who were forced to pay such a disproportionate price for the freedom of their fellow countrymen? What about them and their sacrifices? And particularly those whose sacrifices we now realize with history's hindsight were unnecessary?

One nightmare haunted the men who planned the Allied landings in Normandy. It was the image of a massive, coordinated counter-attack staged by the armoured divisions the Germans had available in France in the first days after the invasion.

If such an attack was carried out with the ruthlessness, the speed, the decisiveness that had characterized so many German actions in the Second World War, there was every reason to fear it would, indeed, drive the Allies back into the waters of the Bay of the Seine.

How to stop the Germans from assembling their forces for such an attack was, therefore, one of the dominating concerns of the Allied planners from early 1944 onwards.

The first major study of the problem was made on February 18, 1944 by the 21st Army Group, the ground commanders who would lead the invasion on February 18, 1944. Of the 10 Panzer divisions the Germans were expected to send to Normandy to wipe out the beachhead, four, the soldiers estimated, would come by rail, four by road, and two by a combination of both.

An immediate plan was set up calling for systematic destruction of key elements of the French railroad system: marshalling yards, round houses, bridges.

Then, for use in the aftermath of D-Day, the planners proposed a wholly new concept—the creation of a series of what they labeled "choke points." A "choke point" would be, in effect, a city. Taken together, those cities would constitute a kind of belt roping off the invasion area.

And what exactly would those "choke points" be? They would be masses of rubble, whatever was left of those unfortunate cities after they had been hammered by a massive bombing attack. By turning those cities into heaps of ruins, the Allied soldiers reasoned, they would make it difficult for the German commanders to move their Panzers through them on their way to the beaches. They would be caught in road jams and bottlenecks that would leave them exposed to attack by Allied fighter-bombers. Those impromptu roadblocks would also force the tank commanders to resort to their wireless sets constantly, thus alerting the Allies as to where they were and making more bombing easier.

A list of towns that would be turned into "choke-points" was appended to that first study. They were: Lisieux, Caen, Bayeux, Saint-Lo, Coutances, and Valognes. It was a stunningly brutal application of air power as a military weapon—and one directed not against the German populations of Hamburg or Dresden, but against the Allies' own French partners.

The plan ran into immediate opposition in Allied circles. First, the attack on the railroads, called the Transportation Plan, was assailed because most of the centers that would have to be attacked were in urban areas and bombing them was bound to cause civilian casualties.

The soldiers, however, led by General Eisenhower, the Supreme Commander, wanted the attacks to go forward. "The greatest contribution the Allied Air Forces could make to Overlord," he said, was to "hinder enemy movement in the invasion's initial phase."

The Air Commanders, and particularly General Carl Andrew Spaatz of the U.S. 8th Air Force, were opposed on the grounds that the attacks would cause an unacceptable number of French casualties.

The matter went up to Winston Churchill. Often in those days the English Prime Minister was depicted as being heedlessly bellicose.

He certainly was not in this matter. He was not convinced, he announced, "the slaughter of masses of friendly French Allies" could be justified. It was one thing, he declared, to launch attacks that would produce civilian casualties "during the hot blood of battle," quite another when no fighting was going on to launch a policy that would result in the butchering of large numbers of French people.

The proposed railway bombings, Churchill declared, risked causing "an unhealable breach between France and the U.S. and Britain in the postwar era."

A revised list of 65 railway targets was selected by the soldiers. Allied planners estimated that they would result in 10,500 French civilians killed and 5,500 seriously wounded.

Again, Churchill objected. In a meeting on April 28 with General Eisenhower, he forced the Supreme Commander to suspend the air attacks on 27 of the targets that were located in the most densely populated areas.

His intervention certainly saved countless lives in those areas. The Normans, alas, were still going pay the wages for their salvation.

On May 10, Field Marshal Sir Bernard Law Montgomery's 21st Army Group submitted to Eisenhower a list of 26 Norman towns the army wanted heavily bombed on June 7 and 8. The term "choke points" had been dropped. Now these towns were described as "nodal" points.

The objective, however, was the same—they were to be converted to mounds of rubble "The highest priority for air attack after D-Day," Montgomery wrote, "should be given to enemy moves through the inner zone close to the bridgehead." The attacks, he estimated, could slow the arrival of the four or five Panzer divisions that would make up the Germans' immediate counter-attacking force. He attached a map to his letter. It showed the 15 towns—"nodal points"—he wanted bombed.

His request drew immediate and serious opposition from the airmen who would be expected to carry it out. General James H. Doolittle of the U.S. 8th Air Force simply refused to have his bombers used as part of the plan.

In a stormy meeting on June 3, Air Chief Marshal Arthur Tedder, and the American generals Spaatz and Doolittle, assailed the plan. Tedder told his fellow Briton, Air Chief Marshal Trafford Leigh-Mallory, the invasion's Air Commander, that he "could not approve this part of the bombing program because of the high civilian casualties likely to be caused as well as the destruction of historic monuments"—casualties and destruction he was not convinced would be offset by whatever the bombings might achieve.

The two Americans supported him.

Leigh-Mallory, however, was adamant in support of the plan. Once the battle was joined, strategic considerations were going to have to be paramount. At all costs the Allied Armies would have to be prevented from being driven back into the sea. There would be civilian casualties, he admitted, but they would be no higher than the casualties the Allied military would have to endure to get ashore. They would be part of the price of France's liberation—a painful part, no doubt, but a justified part as well.

Eisenhower supported him against the airmen. He "emphatically" approved the bombing plan and said he was strongly opposed to holding off from such a vital task because of a reluctance to cause civilian casualties. So intense was the sentiment among the invasion staff in favor of the bombings that Montgomery and Leigh-Mallory even suggested they might resign their commands rather than yield on the plan.

The situation was so delicate that Eisenhower's Deputy Commander, General Walter Bedell Smith, decided to send a delegation of high-ranking Allied officers to General Pierre Koenig, the Commander of the Free French Forces—not to obtain his approval, but to explain what was going to happen and seek, at least, his understanding.

To their intense relief, Koenig understood the military imperatives compelling Eisenhower's headquarters to its decision and raised no objection.

And so those Norman towns were condemned. An effort was made to warn their populations to flee with leaflets scattered two hours before the attacks went in. Some of them fell where they were supposed to. Many were blown into empty fields. Few people could really believe the Allies would bomb their cities. They were not, after all, crawling with German soldiers.

Relentlessly, mercilessly, the bombs came down. In Lisieux the *pompiers* had no water. Fire swept through the old quarters of the city built of wood and masonry, some dating to Gothic times, others to the Renaissance, buildings that had given the city its special cachet.

Miraculously, the cathedral of Ste Thérèse escaped. Villers-Bocage was obliterated. In Vire, the only people moving in the rubble the next morning were German soldiers looting the bombed homes of the city's residents.

A woman outside Saint-Lo saw a copper-colored cloud rising from the city at dawn, smoke from the burning ruins of what had once been one of Normandy's loveliest towns.

"Why did they have to do it?" a woman sitting amidst the ruins of her home in Coutances cried out.

"Etre bombarde par les allies dont nous avons attendu la venu avec tant de ferveur, c'etait si mon propre pere avait tentait de m'etrangler" ecrivait une jeune Normande. ("To be bombarded by the Allies whose coming we had awaited with such fervor, it was as if my own father had strangled me," wrote a young Norman.)

Almost 3,500 Normans lost their lives in those bombings, according to a recent study by Professor Jean Quellien at the University of Caen. Thousands more were

General Marie-Pierre Koenig, Commander of the Free French Forces

left homeless. Even today the scars of those terrible nights remain alive on many a Norman heart, bringing their touch of pain to the otherwise joyful events surrounding D-Day.

Those memories are all the more bitter, those scars deepened by the fact that today we know those Panzer divisions for which so many lovely Norman towns were turned into ruins were never going to arrive.

20.

Fortitude Plays
its Cards

ROUGHLY 60 YEARS AGO, on Thursday June 8, 1944, the Normandy landings entered their most critical phase. Shortly after sunset that night, Major General Leonard T. Gerow, commanding the U.S. Army's 5th Corps at Omaha Beach, the man whose forces represented two-thirds of the Americans committed to the invasion, sent General Eisenhower's headquarters a terse, worried message.

The Allied landings, he said, "were two days behind in reaching their initial objectives, which gives a grave emergency to the situation." The unloading of supplies for his corps coming across the litter of Omaha Beach was already 24 hours behind schedule. The beachhead was everywhere "far short of its desired depth and the entire landing area can still be reached by enemy artillery fire."

And now, he warned Eisenhower, the second phase of the fight was about to begin, the phase that would determine whether or not the Allies would be able to hold onto their bridgehead.

A major German counter-attack had to be expected at any moment, Gerow signaled Eisenhower. It was, after all, what every Allied planner and strategist had foreseen for weeks and months. "The situation is so critical," Gerow bluntly informed the Supreme Commander, "that if this attack comes in, the beachhead will have a very difficult time holding on."

There were that evening 10 Allied divisions, plus some independent tank battalions, ashore. Five more divisions were due to disembark the following day.

That would complete the first phase of the landing. The armada of transports out in the Bay of the Seine would begin steaming back to ports in England and Scotland to take on the supplies and troops of the second wave. Depending on which ports they were sailing to, their turnaround time was going to take three to seven days.

Until they returned, there would be no more reinforcements for the troops ashore. Some of the Allied divisions—the 1st and 29th U.S. and the 3rd Canadian—had been hard hit by heavy fighting. No matter—for the next five to 10 days they were going to have to stand up to whatever the Germans could throw at them.

And they could throw a great deal. During those days, the German High Command would have a minimum of 30 divisions to muster in a counter-attack, more if they followed the dictates of traditional German military strategy and massed all their available forces for an all-out assault.

Thus far only one of the Germans' crack units, the 12th SS Hitler Youth Panzer, had seen action and the results had not been encouraging. In a day of savage fighting, which had seen heavy losses on both sides, those fanatics of the 12th SS had pushed the 3rd Canadian Division back two precious miles into its already constrained beachhead.

The Germans still held the vital crossroads town of Carentan, vital to linking up the two American beaches, Utah and Omaha. The American 1st and British 50th had linked up at Port-en-Bessin, closing one critical gap in the Allied lines. The British division had also captured Bayeux, the only one of the objectives that the Allies had set for themselves on D-Day that was thus far in Allied hands 60 hours after the landings. All along the Allies' slender bridgehead, troops had to be diverted to mopping up German strongpoints that had been bypassed in the first plunge inland on D-Day.

And now the weather was about to change. The break in the Atlantic storm Eisenhower's meteorologists had spotted on the eve of the invasion had run its course;

more bad weather was moving in with all its potential for disrupting the arrival of supplies over the Allied beaches.

Just how seriously the Allied High Command took the warning in General Gerow's words, how real was the threat of a massive German counter-attack driving the Allies back into the sea, is to be measured in the arrival of a distinguished visitor to London that Thursday morning. It was General George C. Marshal, the Chief of Staff of the United States Army, on hand to stand shoulder to shoulder with his British counterparts to "handle any eventuality that might arise."

That was a nice way of saying he would be there to share equally with his British colleagues the blame and criticism in the altogether realistic scenario of the landings turning into a bloody disaster.

Shortly after General Gerow sent his message to Eisenhower, Field Marshal Gerd von Rundstedt convened his evening conference. He was fuming mad. Once again, Rommel, the man he despised as "Marshal Boy Scout" had failed to make any headway against the Allied landing. Furthermore, von Rundstedt was convinced, he wasn't going to with the forces he had at his disposal. "Marshal Boy Scout" had lobbied against von Rundstedt's recommendation to Hitler the evening before to implement Case IIIA, the ruthless stripping of all the reserves out of the Pas-de-Calais for use against the Normandy beachhead.

The Boy Scout wasn't going to get his way tonight, however. So concerned was von Rundstedt at the situation, at the failure to get a massive counter-attack against the Allies organized, that he did something he almost never deigned to do—he invoked his special privilege as a Field Marshal and put in a personal call to Adolf Hitler.

Invoke Case IIIA immediately, this night, he told the Fuhrer. What did it matter whether Normandy was a diversion or the real landing? Only one thing mattered—driving the Allies back into the sea with a massive counter-attack.

A few hours later at his evening strategy conference, Hitler gave in to the old Field Marshal's demands. He issued the one order that might have saved his Reich—implement Case IIIA immediately. Five divisions, including the 116th Panzer, the strongest armoured division in the West, were to start for Normandy as a vanguard of the forces for a major attack. The nightmare that had haunted the imaginings of Eisenhower, Brooke, and every other Allied commander was at hand—the Panzers were coming over the horizon and they were going to be pressing their attack on an Allied beachhead ill-prepared to withstand their onslaught.

If Fortitude, the Allies' carefully-articulated deception plan was going to work, it was going to have to start working right now.

In at least one thing the men who had assembled that plan had been right—their sense of timing. This was the critical juncture at which Hitler would have to make his decision to go all out against the Normandy beachhead. Now theirs was the most daunting of challenges. No one, least of all a dictator, likes to be forced to change his mind, but that is what Fortitude now had to do—make Hitler change his mind about sending those reinforcements to Normandy.

All during the day of June 7 the wireless units imitating the messages of the non-existent First United States Army Group in southeastern England had been sending out an accelerated schedule of messages. After darkness on June 8, those wireless sets suddenly fell silent just as the wireless sets in southwestern England had fallen silent shortly before the Normandy Invasion.

Roman Czerniawski, alias Brutus, the Polish army captain who, thanks to Fortitude, the Germans believed was the Free Polish Air Force liaison to that imaginary army group, radioed his Abwehr controller in Paris that on the evening of June 8 he had spent the day at Dover Castle. From there, he reported he had "seen with my own eyes Army Group Patton preparing to embark at east coast and southeastern English ports." He had even, he told his Abwehr controller, overheard Patton say, "The time has come to commence operations around Calais."

That was the first shot in Fortitude's arsenal.

The second was fired by radio in the nightly reading of the *messages personnels* over the BBC. It came in these words:

"*Message pour la petite Berthe—Salomon a saute ses grandes sabots.* ("Salomon changed his big shoes.")

The first part of that message—the alert phase—was "*Message pour la petite Berthe.*" It had been broadcast along with many others on the night of June 5, the eve of the invasion. It was destined for a group of Resistants somewhere in the area of the Franco-Belgian border.

The network, however, had been penetrated by Abwehr Kommando 307.

Its principal agents had been arrested on June 3.

They had in the course of their interrogation—and one must presume, as a result of torture—given to their captors the two phrases of their "alert" and "action" messages and the significance of each.

The action phrase—"*Salomon a saute ses grandes sabots*"—was to mean a landing would take place in their area along the Franco-Belgian seacoast within 24 hours of the broadcast, and they were to proceed with the sabotage tasks to which they had been assigned.

Who were those Resistants to whom those messages were broadcast? No one knows. The German archives contain the information they revealed to their captors and the interpretation the Germans put on that information. But nowhere is there any indication of who they were, of the names and faces those individuals possessed. The sad presumption must be that they, like so many others, died in the deportation camps.

The sad presumption must also be that London knew their network had been penetrated, that its members were about to be arrested and that they would, in all probability, be forced to reveal those precious phrases to their captors. If the Germans heard the second action phrase broadcast, they would, in view of the way in which they had obtained the information, be expected to accept it at face value, would they not?

The message—for an invasion that was never to be—was broadcast at 1915 Thursday, June 8, 1944.

The third and final shot in Fortitude's arsenal was fired just after midnight by the Spanish double agent, Juan Pujol Garcia, Garbo to the Allies who controlled him, Arabal to the Germans who trusted him. Garbo, as we saw earlier, had been authorized by General Eisenhower to broadcast to his Abwehr controller in Madrid the news that the invasion was coming—*before* the first assault troops had actually landed.

The radio operator in Madrid who received his messages had been away from his post when Garbo was ready to send the Germans that precious bit of intelligence, intelligence designed to make him a prophet in German eyes.

Garbo had exchanged a set of furious messages over the operator's failure with Erich Kuhlenthal, his Abwehr controller. The German had calmed him—and reassured the architects of Fortitude—by promising him a medal and telling him that never had his work been held in such high esteem in Berlin.

And so, shortly after midnight, Garbo's Royal Signal Corps sergeant began to tap out his second, epic message to Madrid. It lasted an extraordinary 122 minutes.

That in itself was an appalling error. It was well known that the German's wireless detection services in Occupied France could locate and arrest a Resistance radio operator transmitting for a fraction of that time. Why wouldn't the Germans have assigned a similar capacity to the English and concluded that their famous agent had to be operating under British control?

For some reason they did not and Garbo's English controllers got away with their egregious mental lapse.

Garbo informed Kuhlenthal that he had summoned his three best sub-agents, men stationed in Sussex, Kent, and East Anglia, to a meeting in London. They had given him a full listing of the units stationed in their areas—the units making up that army of phantoms, the First U.S. Army Group. One told him of landing barges hidden in the Deben and Orwell Rivers behind the Channel Coast, ready to embark troops.

The British had, indeed, planted those barges there just in case the Germans wanted to send a plane over to check on the authenticity of Garbo's message.

From his agents' information, Garbo came to his conclusion. "It is perfectly clear the present attack is a large-scale operation, but diversionary in character for the purpose of establishing a strong bridgehead in order to draw the maximum of our reserves to the area of operation and retain them there so as to be able to strike a blow somewhere else with assured success."

That blow, he suggested, would strike in the Pas-de-Calais, "the shortest route to the object of their illusions, Berlin."

German prisoners of war in a barbed-wire enclosure on Utah Beach, June 6, 1944.

With that, Fortitude had played its last card.

It can very well be said that on that distant June evening, the fate of the Normandy Landings, of an Occupied and bleeding France, of all the rest of Hitler's Europe, hung in the balance.

Would Hitler and his generals swallow the lies that the Allies had so artfully offered them? Or would they ignore them and drive on with the attack which could very well devastate the Allies' beachhead?

21.

Hitler and the Germans Swallow Fortitude's Lie

A TELEPHONE RANG in the headquarters of Field Marshal Gerd von Rundstedt at Saint Germain-en-Laye. It was, according to the log of von Rundstedt's headquarters, 0730 on the morning of June 10, 1944. The caller was Hitler's Chief of Staff, General Alfred Jodl. His call was destined for the elderly Field Marshal.

Von Rundsted, however, was sound asleep. He no longer practiced the early morning rising traditionally associated with his soldiers calling. The call was taken instead by his Operations Officer, Major General Bodo Zimmermann.

Hitler, Jodl told Zimmermann, had received information that made it clear a second Allied landing was about to fall on the Pas-de-Calais. He had taken the decision to cancel his order for Case IIIA, the all-out reinforcement of Normandy. The divisions, the tanks that had been en route to Normandy from the Pas-de-Calais, had been stopped in their tracks and ordered to turn around and return to their positions behind the waters of the English Channel.

That, Zimmermann was to recall, was "the decision that lost the war for Germany."

Hitler and his generals had, as the Anglo-Saxons say, swallowed the greatest lie ever told, the myth of that second Allied Invasion in the Pas-de-Calais, hook, line, and sinker.

How had it happened?

On June 8-9 the planners of the Allied hoax—Operation Fortitude—had planted three key elements of their lie on the German Army's intelligence organization, the Abwehr This is how the Germans reacted to them.

At 0700 Friday June 9, 1944 at the Hotel Lutetia in Paris, in the office of Colonel Oskar Reille, the head of the Abwehr's section IIIF—counter-espionage for the West—found on his desk a report from his Kommando 307. On June 3 this organization had infiltrated, then rounded up a group of Resistants working along the Franco-Belgian border and forced out of them their alert/action messages for the invasion. The action message destined to the group had been broadcast by the BBC at 1915 on June 8. It meant, according to the Resistants who were supposed to receive it, that a landing was due in the Pas-de-Calais area in 24 hours.

Poor Reille. He had pierced the secret of the Normandy landings with that famous Verlaine couplet, *"Les violons longs de l'automne,"* but von Rundstedt's headquarters had dismissed his triumph with the remark that the "Allies weren't going to announce their invasion over the BBC."

Reille wasn't going to let something like that happen with this precious bit of intelligence. He immediately sent off a high priority message, No. 6460/44, to Colonel Alexis von Roenne at *Fremde Heere West*, the Wehrmacht's Intelligence Headquarters for the Western Front.

After analyzing the messages and how they were obtained Reille dismissed the possibility that London could have known their agents had been arrested. The arrests had taken place too recently for that. Instead, he said, "Abwehr IIIF deems it more likely that the announcement actually has to do with a landing operation directed against the Belgian coastline."

At his headquarters at Zossen outside Berlin, Colonel von Roenne agreed. At 1105 on that morning of June 9, 1944, von Roenne personally called Hitler's Intelligence Aide, Colonel Friedrich Adolf Krummacher, at the Fuhrer's headquarters. The meticulous Prussian made a memorandum of their conversation immediately afterwards. It survived the war.

Roenne Krummacher noted that he "attached the greatest importance" to an intercepted radio message to the Resistance revealing "landing operations are to be expected on June 10, which will be directed against the Belgian region." Therefore, von Roenne stressed to Hitler's Aide, "it was out of the question to withdraw troops (from the Pas-de-Calais) to Normandy."

Krummacher was about to leave for Hitler's midday strategy conference. He promised von Roenne he would bring the report to the Fuhrer's attention. Hitler wavered but decided to withhold any final decision until his evening conference. He did, however, order two divisions resting in Poland, the 9th and 10th SS Panzer Divisions, to start back to France immediately.

Von Roenne, with the agreement of Jodl and Keitel, messaged all commands in the West that "In all probability major landing by enemy forces on the Belgian coast is to be expected June 10."

At 1530 that afternoon Jodl called von Rundstedt's headquarters informing the Field Marshal of "a radio intercept indicating the possibility of a second landing tomorrow in the Belgian area." This, Jodl said, "has been brought to the Fuhrer's attention."

Fortitude's cupful of lies was about to overflow. All that was required was just one more drop to send that stream of poisoned information to its ultimate destination, the mind of Adolf Hitler.

That drop reached von Roenne's desk at 2220 June 9. It was, in abbreviated form, the text of the message the Spanish double agent Garbo had radioed to his Abwehr controller in Madrid the night before.

Von Roenne jumped on it. This was it—it was the final proof of the Allies' intentions. He forwarded it by high speed telex to Hitler's headquarters with the following endorsement: "The reports received in the last week from Arabal—the Germans' code name for Garbo—have been confirmed almost without exception and are to be taken as especially valuable."

Eisenhower's risk in letting Garbo tell Madrid the invasion was coming before the troops had landed had been more than justified. Krummacher endorsed von Roenne's conclusion and handed Garbo's message to Jodl. Jodl in turn passed it to Hitler and a notation in green ink on the document, discovered after the war, establishes the fact Hitler, indeed, read it.

Some of the notes of that night's strategy conference survived the war as well. "The German forces presently engaged in Normandy," they concluded, "will not be sufficient to throw back into the sea the enemy forces which have landed—yet this is the foundation of the conduct of operations in the West and the further strategic conduct of the war."

Having set out that basic concept, the conference than took a 180-degree turn away from it. "Because of the uncertainty as to where Patton's armies will attack, it is not yet possible to quickly reinforce the combat front in

Normandy by appreciably weakening our forces in the 15th Army sector. A rapid enemy success on the Channel or Belgian coasts will bring about the collapse of the entire defense in the West."

And there was undoubtedly another concern in Hitler's mind that night. The opening of his rocket attack on England from his V-bomb bases had been set for June 12. The Allies would be compelled to strike the Pas-de-Calais to stop that rain of high explosives, wouldn't they?

In any event, at 0130 Saturday, June 10, 1944, Hitler changed his mind. He cancelled Case IIIA. The 500 tanks and 50,000 German troops already moving towards Normandy were ordered to stop their advance and return to their positions in the Pas-de-Calais.

At midday that Saturday morning, General George Marshal, the Chief of Staff of the U.S. Army, Field Marshal Sir Alan Brooke, Chief of the Imperial General Staff, and an assortment of high-ranking Allied officers gathered in the operations room of Churchill's underground headquarters at Storey's Gate in London to follow the situation in Normandy.

Sir Ronald Wingate, the Deputy Head of the LCS, the London Controlling Section responsible for Operation Fortitude, recorded the scene in his memoirs after the war. He described the tensions as they watched the red arrows indicating the German reinforcements flowing towards the Allies' exposed bridgehead.

Suddenly the secretary responsible for the Top Secret Ultra intercepts of the Germans' radio messages came into the room. She had just logged an important message into the Black Book that contained vital intercepts. Hitler, it revealed, had abruptly cancelled Case IIIA.

"We knew than that we'd won," Wingate exulted. "There might be heavy battles ahead, but we'd won."

A few minutes later a triumphant Winston Churchill strode in and pronounced the success of Fortitude "the crowning achievement in the long and glorious history of the British Secret Service."

And indeed it was. For the next eight weeks the 15th German Army, the best army the Nazis possessed, would remain frozen in place in the Pas-de-Calais, its cannon unfired, its troops unblooded, waiting for an invasion that was never going to take place to be staged by an army that had never existed.

The road ahead, as Wingate had noted, would be long and painful. The fighting in Normandy, from hedgerow to hedgerow, from field to field, in the ruins of Saint-Lo and Caen, would be as bitter as any in the West in the Second World War. For some of the units involved there, both Allied and German, it would be the only time in which their casualties would compare with those of the terrible battles of the First World War.

For the civilians of Normandy, the price would be high, too—many of them would be called on to pay in blood and shattered homes the price of the liberation of their countrymen elsewhere in France.

But there is no doubt—from the moment of that phone call from Hitler's headquarters to Saint Germain-en-Laye—the success of the Normandy Landings, of the coming liberation of France, and, ultimately, the defeat of Nazi Germany, was a certainty.

U.S. Soldiers of the 8th Infantry Regiment, 4th Infantry Division, move out over the seawall on Utah Beach, after coming ashore. Other troops are resting behind the concrete wall.